# INSURANCE PRICING AND LOSS PREVENTION

*To Ann*

# Insurance pricing and loss prevention

NEIL DOHERTY

SAXON HOUSE | LEXINGTON BOOKS

*Published by*

SAXON HOUSE, D.C. Heath Ltd.
Westmead, Farnborough, Hants., England


*Jointly with*

LEXINGTON BOOKS, D.C. Heath & Co.
Lexington, Mass. USA

| HG | Doherty, Neil A. |
| 8065 | |
| .D63 | Insurance pricing |
| 1976 | and loss prevention |
| 368.015 D6 | |

ISBN 0 347 01097 0
Library of Congress Catalog Card Number 76—9188
Printed in Great Britain by Biddles Ltd. of Guildford

# Contents

**List of tables**

# List of figures

# Foreword

The relationship between loss prevention and insurance is both fascinating and relatively unexplored. As the leading insurance companies increase their involvement in this field I have been struck by the potential absurdity of the company so successful in its encouragement of its policyholders to adopt the ultimate means of avoiding risk that it left itself with nothing to insure.

Unlikely though this may be, the relationship between the two roles of the insurance industry has never been fully explored. Neil Doherty's research, leading to the publication of this book, makes a unique contribution.

A paradox just as difficult to explain is the reticence of the insurance industry in the UK, rightly known for its pioneering work in so many fields, to encourage and to foster links with the universities. Nottingham has established a special reputation and I am delighted that the first insurance-sponsored Fellowship at a British university should have lead to the publication of this book.

David Rowland
*Managing Director,*
*Stewart Wrightson (UK) Ltd*

# Preface

We live in a safety conscious age. Legislation designed to reduce or eliminate the waste of human, capital and natural resources is becoming pervasive and the spread of the risk management philosophy in firms has focussed attention on loss prevention as an alternative strategy to insurance for handling risks. In these days, there is much talk about whether insurance companies should move into the loss prevention business. The traditional approach of insurers has not concerned itself with whether a risk can be improved or not but simply with the rating and underwriting of risks.

Despite the topicality of the question, there is one vital sense in which insurers have always been in the loss prevention business. The very fact of insurance does not have neutral implications for loss prevention; the insurance contract is surrounded by a complex set of financial incentives which may influence or determine attitudes towards loss prevention. It is the study of this interface between insurance and loss prevention which has been chosen for the first Stewart Wrightson Research Fellowship at the University of Nottingham.

There are many people who have offered help and good advice to whom my thanks are due. Perhaps I might be forgiven for singling out three to whom I owe a particular debt: David Rowland, without whose enthusiasm this project would never have taken off; Gordon Sanders, whose good sense and insight provided a link between the theoretical approach and the real world; and Professor Bob Carter, to whom my intellectual debt is such that I am never quite sure which are my own ideas and which are his.

Finally, my thanks must go to my wife and children whose love and patience make it all possible and worthwhile.

Neil A. Doherty
March 1976

# 1 Introduction

One of the notable developments in insurance over the last few years has been the spread of risk management techniques. This development has drawn attention away from the idea that insurance is a necessary instrument for handling risk to a more comprehensive approach in which insurance is seen only as one of a number of competing strategies. Risks may be retained, avoided, reduced or transferred, or some combination of these strategies may be adopted. But perhaps the most significant contribution of risk management has been the stress it has placed on the interdependence between these strategies. If there is any financial interdependence between, say, the transfer of risk and the reduction of risk, then it is appropriate to take account of this interdependence in formulating an optimal risk management programme. This introduces not only the possibility that the protection of the risk might provide a more cost effective alternative to insurance but also the possibility that the insurance cover might determine what type and degree of protection is required.

Whilst the idea of substitution between insurance and loss prevention on the basis of interdependent incentives might be explained as rational economic behaviour on the part of the insured, the same relationship introduces rather disturbing problems from the viewpoint of the insurer. It is normally a precondition for underwriting that risks can be identified and, to some degree, measured. This permits calculations of an appropriate premium and the pooling of a large number of such risks will help the insurer to achieve a stable and satisfactory financial performance. The first disturbing feature is that the relationship between insurance and loss prevention suggests that the risk 'mutates' once it is insured and consequently the premium might turn out to be inadequate. If this change in the risk is predictable and observable, then it might be accounted for in the insurer's calculations and the conditions of cover, but if it is simply a change in the attitudes and behaviour of the insured, then the insurer might find himself biting off more than he can chew.

This problem arises because it is the insured who bears the costs and inconvenience of loss prevention and who is in control of those factors which influence the degree of risk. However, since the risk is transferred under the contract of insurance, he is relieved of the financial burden of loss. It is the insurer who pays for the losses and thereby benefits from loss prevention, but he may not be in a position to enforce decisions on

1

protection. The transfer of risk is not accompanied by a transfer of property rights. Thus in motor insurance, the insured may determine the choice of car, the speed and care with which he drives, the standard of maintenance and repair of his car and the use of safety features such as seat belts and head rests. Of course, other factors remain beyond his control, such as the driving habits of others, the weather conditions and the state of repair of the highway, but even then, a defensive and adaptible attitude towards driving may limit his exposure to these external factors. Since insurance relieves the financial burden of motor accidents, there may be some concern about the adverse incentives which it introduces, though excessive alarm may be dispelled if high standards of safety are imposed through traffic regulations and instincts for survival. With property insurance, there may be less complacency. Insurance effectively insulates the owner of property from the financial effects of loss and so there is no financial gain to be made from incurring the expense and inconvenience of protecting his property. The benefit from loss prevention is transferred to the insurer.

One aspect of the adverse relationship between risk transfer and incentives for loss prevention which has been given wide attention is moral hazard. In one sense, moral hazard refers to abuses of insurance protection which relate to deficiency of character on the part of the insured, for example, faking a claim or exaggerating its amount or even deliberate destruction of property in order to claim the insurance money. 'Some of these abuses are fraudulent; others indicate a different (and indefensible) code of ethics where insurance is concerned.'[1] A broader interpretation, sometimes called morale hazard, refers to factors such as carelessness and indifference which may not suggest moral deficiency but still refer to personality traits which react with the security of insurance protection.

The focus of moral hazard is narrow and emotive; it directs our attention only to the tainted and the neglectful. This is not very helpful to a systematic discussion of the effects of insurance on loss prevention since it sidetracks from other aspects of the relationship which may be even more important and which have largely been ignored. Suppose an insured considers whether to instal a sprinkler system to protect his factory. Acting rationally, he evaluated all the costs and benefits which include *inter alia* the effects of the installation on the terms of his insurance protection. Can we assume there is a moral, or morale, hazard simply because his decision on protection may depend on whether he is insured? In fact, there may be a stronger argument that since such rational decisionmaking is conducive to economic efficiency, it will increase social welfare and it would be 'immoral' not to consider the terms of insurance protection when making

2

the decision. Clearly, the discussion of morality is confusing and irrelevant and in what follows an entirely neutral view of the effects of insurance incentives is adopted.

Whilst the contract of insurance transfers incentives for loss prevention to the insurer, it is rarely accompanied by a corresponding right to interfere with the insured's life, activity or property. There is a separation of incentive and control. Nevertheless, the insurer is not without bargaining power since he may vary the terms and conditions on which he goes on cover. There may be a system of premium reductions and/or extensions of cover if the insured does specific things to reduce the risk. Alternatively, there may be premium penalties, exclusions of cover or threatened withdrawal of cover altogether in the face of adverse features of the risk. A third possibility is that insurance premiums may be directly related to claims experience such that bad risks will, on average, pay more for their insurance than good risks. It is therefore clear that the pricing of insurance and the conditions of cover may create a system of secondary incentives for loss prevention such that insureds who reduce their expected claims costs are rewarded by a premium reduction and those whose claims costs rise will be penalised in the premium structure.

The overall effect which insurance has on loss prevention depends largely upon whether these premium incentives can adequately restore the financial stake which the insured has in losses. At worst, the insurer will be unable to monitor the expected claims cost for the insured and how this changes as he modifies his behaviour and incorporates safety devices. Thus he will be unable to include incentives for insurance protection in the insurance contract. At best, the insurer will have perfect information and the conditions of cover will be finely tuned to reflect changes in the degree of risk.

If we consider how the insured responds to these incentives, it is important that we look not only at the information available to the insurer, but also at how well informed the insured is of the consequences of his actions. Without insurance, the individual may be quite unaware of the various safety measures which he may adopt to reduce his risk, but even if he is aware, the problems of measuring the benefits of loss prevention are immense. He has to take account of the estimated probability that a loss will occur, the range of values it can assume if it does occur and how these values change with different loss prevention programmes. For the individual, such a task is formidable, yet the insurers are assembling this information and translating it into differentials in their premium rating structures in the everyday course of their business. For the individual who is insured, decisions on safety and loss prevention are simplified largely to

3

a comparison of the cost of loss prevention and the appropriate reduction in insurance premium. In this way insurance pricing disseminates information on loss prevention and, assuming the premiums accurately reflect the costs which each insured imposes on the insurance fund, thereby improves the basis for decisionmaking.

The policy implications which arise from the relationship between insurance and loss prevention turn out to be important. There is considerable alarm over the volume of resources, both human and non-human, which are impaired or destroyed by fires, explosions, floods, road accidents, industrial injuries and the like. Whilst, for reasons of economic efficiency, it may not be desirable to eliminate these losses, it is important that an appropriate balance is attained between the marginal value of the resources destroyed and the marginal value of resources allocated to loss prevention. But since decisions on loss prevention are made by individuals it is not certain that this overall balance will be reached. The result will depend upon the economic system in which these decisions are made. Thus if the costs and benefits of loss prevention are borne by the same individuals, then their private decisions may lead to an efficient allocation of resources. With insurance, however, there is a complex process by which incentives are transferred between the various parties to the contract and new incentives are created. It therefore becomes important to examine insurers' pricing systems to see whether they do imply an efficient distribution of the burden of claims. If this is not achieved, there may well be a welfare case for public intervention in some form such as the stimulation of information flows or the dissolution of monopolistic groupings of insurers.

The issues are equally important for other groupings. For insurers, the ultimate success of a loss prevention campaign would drive them out of business. Whilst this extreme situation may not be plausible, a more modest reduction in losses may have ambiguous effects for insurers' profits since it will tend to reduce both premiums and claims. It therefore becomes clear that if insurers are to achieve their optimal commercial strategy, they must take into account the interdependence between their pricing structure and the level of claims costs imposed on the insurance fund. It is particularly important that this interdependence is understood by insurers who are contemplating horizontal diversification into the loss prevention business. Whilst the provision of loss prevention services may bring its own income, it will also have spillover effects in terms of the profits from insurance operations. The compatibility of these two operations cannot, as is so often assumed, be taken for granted.

For insureds, the welfare implications of the interdependence between insurance and loss prevention can be analysed in terms of a series of

4

subsidies between different risk groups. An insurance pricing system which fails to achieve an efficient distribution of claims costs is, in effect, creating a system of subsidies between high and low risk insureds. These subsidies are not only important for reasons of equity but may also interfere with an efficient allocation of resources.

Whilst the relationship between insurance and loss prevention is of obvious interest to those involved in the day-to-day transaction of insurance business, it is also of interest to the applied economist. The logical content of the relationship is not so very different from many other policy situations encountered by economists and for which he has at his fingertips a body of conceptual analysis from which policy recommendations can be formulated. Two examples in which economic analysis has been widely used reveal the basic parallels and show the potential value of an economic interpretation of the insurance/loss prevention problem. The recent concern with ecology has drawn economists into the study of pollution and economic analysis has undoubtedly made an impact on government thinking. More traditionally, economists have been involved in the formulation of pricing policy for public enterprises and, whilst a simple solution has proved illusive, the underlying analysis does throw light on the problems encountered in the present study.

The current concern with pollution arises largely (though not exclusively: there is also concern with the rate of depletion of natural resources) from a conflict between different interest groups. These groups are identified most easily as those whose activities generate smoke, noise, effluent or other forms of pollution and those who suffer from pollution in terms of increases in the costs of undertaking their own (different) activities or in terms of general annoyance or inconvenience. The policy options available to governments include the regulation by fiat or financial controls which re-align the costs of pollution. Thus the pollutee might be granted freedom at law to discharge effluent; or have had his freedom curtailed by the imposition of an obligation to compensate those who suffer; or be subject to a tax liability for the pollution he discharges; or be banned from undertaking the activity altogether.

The essential feature of the pollution problem is that the costs of the activity may not be borne by the party who controls and profits by the activity. This is precisely the source of concern in the insurance/loss prevention problem. Consequently, the body of analysis developed by economists for the regulation of pollution and the resolution of the conflicting interests of those who profit and suffer is clearly of relevance.

The second area in which the economist's skills have had productive use is with the pricing policies of public enterprises. Unlike a private company,

5

it is not self-evident that the public enterprise is in business to reap the maximum attainable level of profits. Whilst the management decisions of private enterprises have traditionally been seen to be geared to the interests of shareholders (though with employee interests acting as an important constraint) public enterprise decisions are presumed to be based upon a wider notion of the public interest. Although the public interest is never clearly and unambiguously defined, it must involve some balance of the conflicting interests of various social groups in a democratic society. Thus whilst the owners of the public enterprise (taxpayers) have a direct interest in high levels of profit, the consumers are more interested in low prices. But whilst these groups are important, they do not exhaust the public interest. Wider implications may be seen with the impact of the public enterprise pricing policy on the activities of competing enterprises and upon the use made of the nation's scarce resources. Whilst the economist *per se* is not qualified to place values on these competing claims over income and wealth, he may be able to identify the nature and magnitude of the conflict and to help devise strategies which reflect the values which are given by the political process. For example, if it were decided that taxpayers' interests should be dominant, then the optimal price would just balance incremental revenue with incremental costs. Alternatively, a policy in which the public enterprise just breaks even (average cost pricing) might be seen as an appropriate balance between the conflicting interests of consumers and taxpayers. A third alternative might be needed if it is decided that the public interest is best served if the pricing decision reflects part of a wider economic strategy which is designed to put the nation's scarce resources to their most productive use – possibly a marginal cost pricing strategy.

The relevant features of these two examples are that situations in which there is a separation of the control of an activity and the cost bearing resulting from that activity have been fruitfully analysed by economists. Furthermore, the conflicts which arise from economic activities often depend upon the pricing policies adopted; both the level of the activity and the nature of the conflicting interests can often be manipulated by use of pricing policy. The overlap between these problems and the insurance/loss prevention issues outlined earlier are clear but there is still one important element missing.

The important feature which is missing in these examples is risk and uncertainty. Here, the economist's credentials are ambiguous. Interest in risk and uncertainty has had a long but somewhat lonely evolution. It can be traced back largely to Daniel Bernoulli in the eighteenth century and his central theorems have led to a slowly blossoming interest in the subject.

In spite of this, the mainstream of economic theory has developed largely on the assumption that we live in a world which is free from risk. It is often assumed that our knowledge (sometimes including our knowledge of the future) is without limit. This conflict is now being resolved mainly on the theoretical plane with the allocation of intellectual resources to the task of re-formulating traditional theory to take account of risk and uncertainty: often with startling results. The practical relevance of this development rests upon the validity of the theorist's assumptions, in particular that of the rationality of the participants.

The main theoretical emphasis in looking into risk and uncertainty has been to display the behaviour of the consistent and rational economic man. Thus Bernoulli proposed that a man who was averse to risk (meaning that he would prefer a certain money outcome to a risky prospect with the same mathematical value, i.e. £1 would be preferred to a 50 per cent chance of £2) would by definition purchase insurance when the premium was equal to the expected value of the risk. On the other hand, he would refuse to gamble at equally fair odds. A whole series of more subtle theorems have been developed but the operational value of these is limited by the assumption that the actors behave rationally and that they are able to evaluate the risks which they face. These limitations are also reflected in much of the conceptual analysis of this book. Whilst the validity of these assumptions must be in doubt when considering individual insurance purchasers the assumptions may have growing validity in the case of corporate insureds. The spread of risk management techniques certainly reflects a systematic attempt amongst insureds to identify and evaluate their risks and to formulate a co-ordinated strategy which takes account of the interdependencies between insurance and loss prevention.

The purpose of this book is to build an economic model of the relationships between insurers' pricing systems and loss prevention from which these issues can be examined. The model is constructed in three stages. In chapter 2 the behavioural responses of insureds to the financial incentives of insurance contracts is examined. These responses will depend on the pricing strategies adopted by insurers. In chapter 3 these pricing strategies are themselves examined in the light of insurers' objectives and the state of competition in the market for insurance services. The third stage of the model relates to the creation and flow of information. On the one hand, accurate information on loss probabilities is a prerequisite for an efficient pricing structure; on the other hand, the response of the insured to premium incentives depends upon this information being conveyed to him. Chapter 4 examines whether the rating structures adopted by insurers and the institutions within the insurance market can disseminate appropriate information on loss probabilities.

From this economic framework, the structure and development of two particular insurance markets is examined. Chapter 5 analyses the fire insurance market, the rating systems which have emerged and their implications for fire prevention. A comparative study of motor insurance practice is undertaken in chapter 6. Chapter 7 considers the overall context within which decisions on loss prevention are made and places the insurance effects within a wider list of costs and benefits of loss prevention. The implications for social policy, together with the policy issues facing both insurers and insureds are then discussed in the final chapter.

**Note**

[1] C.A. Williams and R.M. Heins, *Risk Management and Insurance,* McGraw Hill 1964, p.51.

# 2  Risk management, insurance and loss prevention

The example of pollution was used in the previous chapter to highlight the interest of economists in what are known as externalities or external costs. The literature on this subject is now adapted to the insurance situation to analyse the consequences for loss prevention and to identify, at least in general terms, remedies for any misdirection of resources. This will require a brief look at externalities on a somewhat theoretical level.

## Externalities

An externality may be said to exist when the activities of one person impose costs or benefits upon others. This may occur at a purely subjective level (I am happy at your success) but more importantly for present purposes it may occur at a monetary level. The activities of one person, A, may affect the actual or potential level of income or wealth of another, B. Common examples are: (i) the smoke from A's chimney damages neighbour B's washing; (ii) effluent discharged by factory A damages farmer B's crop; and (iii) the use of a motor car by A imposes risk of injury (and consequent loss of income etc.) to pedestrian B. Issues such as these are of immense importance for social welfare and public policy. Much of the common law system reflects an attempt to re-allocate the costs of such events and the ongoing debate about pollution reflects concern about the way in which a certain class of external costs happens to fall. An analogous problem is created with the transfer of rights under an insurance policy. The activities of one party to the contract affect the level of costs which are to be picked up by the other party. Subsequent sections of this chapter will adapt the general literature to the insurance situation.

The essential ingredients of the externality problem can be reduced to a single diagram. In Fig. 2.1 the line *FG* measures the marginal gain, (the additional gain for each additional unit of the activity which is undertaken) to A which arises from a particular activity.[1] However, the activity also imposes external costs upon a second individual B such that his marginal loss (additional loss for each extra unit of the activity undertaken by A) is represented by the line *HJ*. The ideal level of activity for A is at *OG* since

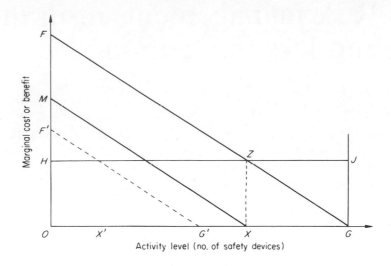

Fig. 2.1   The optimal level of loss prevention

he will thereby maximise his gain. The gain can be identified as the area under *FG*. If A is given unrestricted freedom to undertake the activity he may be expected to arrive at level *OG*. The optimum for B, however, is achieved when A undertakes zero units of the activity and B thus suffers no loss. One way to resolve the conflict is to add A's gain and B's loss and maximise this sum to achieve a 'social optimum'. This will be achieved at that level of the activity at which A's marginal gain equals B's marginal loss. This gives activity level *OX*. It may be thought that the proper function of government is to see whether economic forces will lead to this point, or, if they do not, to intervene in the market to ensure that the optimum is achieved. Alternatively, the government may think it proper to attach some form of weighting to A's gain schedule and B's loss schedule in accordance with its income distribution objectives. However, it is more convenient here to allocate a neutral weighting and to consider the social optimum as the simple sum of A's gain and B's loss.

In theory, at least, the social optimum may be achieved if the parties to the externality are free to bargain. If A has legal and financial freedom to undertake the activity, then it will pay B to offer money to A in order to persuade him to reduce his activity level from *OG* to *OX*. Any sum between *XZG* and *XZJG* will result in mutual gain since it will be lower than the reduction in B's loss from the reduction in the activity level, *XZJG*, but higher than the reduction in A's gain from reducing the level of

10

activity, $XZG$. Alternatively, if the law states that A can only undertake the activity with B's permission, then it can also be shown to be of mutual benefit for A to purchase such permission in order to operate at activity level $OX$. These solutions have been analysed in detail elsewhere[2] and probably make unusual demands on both the rationality and knowledge of the parties to be altogether credible. Furthermore, they are of less interest in the insurance context than solutions which occur through a form of pricing.

If A is required to fully compensate B for any loss suffered, then his gain will be reduced by the amount of compensation paid. In diagrammatic terms, A's net gain is now shown by curve $MX$ which is the vertical difference between his original marginal gain curve and the marginal loss imposed upon B. Now A will maximise his gain (the area under $MX$) by producing at activity level $OX$. An alternative way of achieving the same result is for the State to impose a pollution tax. If the marginal tax rate is equal to B's marginal loss for each level of the activity, line $HJ$, then A will again maximise his gain at $OX$.

This analysis can now be transferred to the insurance situation. This requires that the activity be re-defined and that the concepts of gain and loss from the activity be re-interpreted accordingly. There are alternative ways in which this can be done. One approach is to define the activity in the same way as in the externalities example, i.e. as something which is pursued for financial or economic gain. The benefit is then obvious and the costs can be considered as those losses which are transferred under the insurance contract. However, a more helpful approach is to define the activity as loss prevention and to define its cost as the opportunity cost (disrupted production from following safety codes or increased time spent in slow and safe driving) or the price paid for the loss prevention device. The benefit requires slightly more attention. This is the reduction in the probability of loss and/or the reduction in the size of the contingent loss. In order to translate this into a two-dimensional diagram it is necessary to consider the benefit as a single value. In theoretical terms the appropriate measure would be the utility value which would be placed upon this benefit by the person on whom it falls. However, since this value is difficult, if not impossible, to identify, and would in any case vary between individuals, it is easier to use some objective measure. The measure chosen is therefore the reduction in the expected value of loss.

Returning to Fig. 2.1, the horizontal axis now measures the degree of loss prevention. This might be measured as the number of sprinklers, the reduction in driving speed, employee days spent on safety education etc. (Alternatively, loss prevention could be measured simply in terms of total expenditure in which case the marginal cost curve would be a horizontal line by definition). Line *HJ* measures the marginal cost of loss prevention which is borne by the insured and line *FG* measures the reduction in the expected value of losses which is brought about by incremental units of loss prevention. The socially optimal level of expenditure on loss prevention is now found by maximising the surplus of benefits over costs. The net marginal gain curve is *MX* and the optimal activity level is *OX*. Without insurance, this would also be the privately optimal level of loss prevention since costs and benefits would fall on the same party. However, with insurance, the benefits of loss prevention are transferred to the insurer and the privately optimal level for the insured is now zero since he can thereby avoid all expenditure on loss prevention. (A more formal model is presented in the appendix to this chapter and this is extended to verify the main theorems of the chapter.)

The shift in the rational level of loss prevention with the introduction of insurance is developed in the rest of this chapter. First, a further point of contrast may be made with the pollution case. With pollution the regulation of the activity by means of some form of financial or legal control was achieved through external intervention. However, with insurance the parties are in a contractual relationship which is secured by the payment of an agreed premium. This internal device provides a potential mechanism for regulating expenditure on loss prevention and its role is developed in the next chapter.

### Two concepts of moral hazard

Moral hazard has been described as '. . . every deviation from correct human behaviour that may pose a problem for an insurer.'[3] This interpretation, which is in popular usage, focusses upon ethical factors which affect the degree of risk. It stresses the insured's character and the role this will play in determining loss probabilities. This may be very useful in putting underwriters on guard before accepting risks but its lack of precision makes it difficult to use in an economic analysis of insurance and loss prevention.

An alternative concept of moral hazard focusses not on 'moral perfidy but [on] rational economic behaviour'.[4] This approach is highlighted by M.V. Pauly[5] and can be illustrated simply by considering the demand for medical care. The marginal cost of a standard unit of medical care is given by the curve *CC* in Fig. 2.2 and the demand for medical services, given a (standardised) illness, is shown by the curve *DD*. If the individual

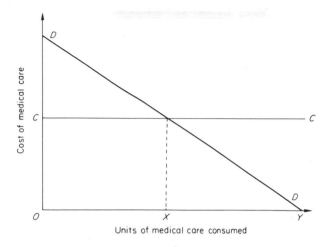

Fig. 2.2　Optimal expenditure on medical care

does not insure, he has to pay a marginal cost of $OC$ per unit of medical care and he consumes $OX$ units. If he is insured, the marginal cost of medical care is zero and he consumes $OY$ units. Increased consumption of medical care under insurance protection is seen as a rational response to economic incentives.

In this example loss prevention would take the form of mitigation of the size of loss but this does not occur since it has a cost for the insured, i.e. the sacrifice of benefits which are available at zero price. The failure to mitigate loss is conceptually similar to the more obvious case where loss prevention takes the form of *ex ante* behaviour to avoid or reduce loss. With both interpretations of loss prevention there has been a reduction in the level which is privately optimal and this has been caused by the introduction of insurance.

Some writers have distinguished between *moral* hazard, which '. . . is a subjective characteristic of the insured that increases the probability of loss' and which '. . . arises when insureds' create a loss to collect their insurance policies', and *morale* hazard, which '. . . is presented by the ordinary insured who does not seek to protect his property or who is careless because he is insured.'[6] The rational concept considered here more closely resembles morale hazard, though the focus of this study is concerned with the economic incentives created by a system of insurance and the insured's response to them. The use of the term 'moral hazard' is without any ethical undertones – the insured's response to economic incentives is considered to be morally neutral.

13

## Moral hazard and indemnity

In the medical care example, the marginal cost of medical services to the insured person was zero and, in the second example, the expected payback from safety devices for the insured person was zero. These two conditions imply first, that the insured will be fully compensated for his financial loss and, secondly, that the insurance premium does not discriminate between good and bad risks. The first of these conditions is examined here and the second occupies the following section. The principle of full compensation is known as indemnity and underlies most insurance contracts. The legal effect of indemnity is that the insured should receive no financial gain nor suffer any financial loss from the insured event.[7] Consequently in pecuniary terms the insured will be indifferent as to whether the insured event occurs or not and receives no financial benefit from avoiding losses.

Most property and liability policies are contracts of indemnity[8] since the loss can usually be subjected to objective evaluation. The prices prevailing in property/commodity markets offer objective indicators of the value of destroyed property and, in liability claims, the valuation of the loss is determined by the court or agreed in out of court bargaining. In other situations there are few indicators which would provide an objective evaluation of loss, and here the principle of indemnity is displaced either by an agreement to pay a predetermined sum for a given event or a clear unambiguous formula for calculation of loss is specified in the policy. Life and personal accident insurance fall into this category.

The analysis here is mainly concerned with contracts of indemnity and is therefore directly relevant to most property and liability insurances. This gets rid of the more difficult problems which arise when economic markets offer no objective valuation of the size of loss. However, the objective valuations which may be inferred for property and liability insurance are not unambiguous. There are several possible interpretations of indemnity each of which has its own implications for loss prevention. These complications lead from the more general case that insurance might relax incentives for loss prevention to the more dramatic case that insurance might create incentives to induce loss.

Indemnity requires that the insured is restored to the same financial position that he occupied immediately before the loss. But the term 'financial position' is not capable of unique measurement if part of the assets are held in a non-liquid form. For example, how should the property be valued? At the price which could be obtained by re-sale on secondhand markets or at the cost of re-purchase of similar property on the second-hand market? These two valuations differ by the transaction costs and the

14

profits of traders operating in secondhand markets and this difference can be substantial in some markets. However, the problems do not stop here. What if no secondhand market exists or exists only in a very imperfect form such that it is only a matter of chance whether the buyers, traders and sellers come into contact? Hence secondhand prices may not exist or may vary according to those particular contacts that happen to be established through chance. In these situations, does the cost of replacing with new property offer the appropriate measure of indemnity? These problems have certainly defied a general solution in the insurance world.

If indemnity implies a state of indifference between the position of the insured immediately before his loss and his position immediately after insurance settlement, then the choice between competing measures should ideally rest upon the intentions of the individual concerned. This can most easily be illustrated by example. Two individuals, A and B, have identical assets. These assets can be divided between liquid assets (cash, bank deposits and easily redeemable securities) and non-liquid assets (property). Individual A is not satisfied with the division of his assets between liquid and non-liquid: he would prefer to convert his non-liquid assets into cash. On the other hand, B is perfectly satisfied with his current division of assets: he prefers to retain his non-liquid assets rather than sell them off at going secondhand prices. Both are insured and suffer a complete loss of their respective non-liquid assets. The implications of the different interpretations of indemnity can now be plotted by comparing (a) each person's assets before the loss and the available market opportunities for interchanging between liquid and non-liquid assets with (b) the asset structure after the insurer had made good the loss with a financial settlement. We can examine whether settlement according to the different criteria of the previous paragraph leaves the insureds better off or worse off in terms of their identified preferences over liquid and non-liquid assets. This is shown in the following tabulation:

| | Criterion for measurement of loss | | |
| --- | --- | --- | --- |
| | Re-sale value secondhand | Replacement cost secondhand | Replacement cost new |
| A | Indifferent | Gain | Gain |
| B | Loss | Indifferent | Gain |

Thus individual A would prefer to sell off non-liquid assets for cash but before he can do so a loss occurs. If he is paid the re-sale value secondhand he has neither gained nor lost from the loss since he wished to sell at this price anyway. An insurance settlement on the basis of the replacement cost, however, effectively permits him to 'sell off' assets at a rate which was unobtainable to him before the loss. Individual B, however, is left indifferent by a settlement on the secondhand replacement cost basis. In consistency with his preferences, he will simply go out and replace what he has lost, thereby reverting to his pre-loss asset position.

More formally, the types of losses which may be suffered may be classified as follows. First, the loss of opportunities for disposing of property at the re-sale secondhand value and, secondly, the transaction costs which may be incurred in establishing a new preferred asset mix. These losses may or may not be insured. Criterion 1, re-sale value secondhand, insures losses of the first type quite independently of individual preferences but does not cover losses of the second type. Whether this involves a welfare loss on the part of the insured depends upon his asset preferences. In contrast, criterion 2, replacement cost secondhand, insures these transaction costs regardless of the insured's asset preferences. Thus those who wish to re-purchase property after the loss are neither better nor worse off but those who prefer to hold cash receive a windfall gain from the insurance settlement. Criterion 3, replacement cost new, covers both types of loss in addition to something that has not been lost. This results in an unambiguous welfare gain regardless of the individual's preferences.

These considerations of indemnity and individual preference lead to a different type of relationship between insurance and loss prevention to that set out for this study. Where indemnity is based on replacement cost (new or secondhand) then some or all insureds have a positive incentive to induce loss. Such behaviour is clearly fraudulent and consequently subject to a quite different set of sanctions to the economic controls set out in this book. These considerations are far beyond the present study and to focus attention on the main subject matter indemnity will be defined to imply that the insured is restored to a state which yields equal satisfaction to that which prevailed immediately before the loss.

## Moral hazard and premium rating

### Premium incentives

The 'externalities' view of the insurance transaction stresses the transfer of financial incentives to avoid loss from the insured to the insurer, but reveals the impotency of the insurer to act upon these incentives. This lack of control may be made good by the terms and conditions the insurer may impose on the insurance contract. First, the financial incentives which are removed from the insured may be restored if the insurer quotes premiums which discriminate according to the degree of protection. Secondly, the insurer may simply refuse to underwrite a risk unless a certain safety device is installed or a particularly hazardous feature removed. The maxim that 'there is a rate for every risk', suggests that this second case really simplifies into a rating problem. Underwriters will often quote high premiums rather than decline a risk and, even if one underwriter will not accept, the worst risk can usually be placed at some price by shopping around.

## Rational expenditure on loss prevention

The level of expenditure on loss prevention which is optimal for the individual may be defined as that level which equates the marginal costs and marginal benefits. The dominating costs are the direct and opportunity costs of installing and maintaining safety devices and/or the costs of altering behaviour in such a way as to reduce the probability or severity of loss. The principal benefits of loss prevention are the reduction in the cost of uninsured losses and/or the reduction in insurance premiums, depending on whether, and how much, insurance is purchased. The schedule of costs and benefits may be disturbed by other factors such as taxation and grants on capital expenditure and, for present purposes, it may be assumed that costs and benefits are specified net of these factors. In comparing costs and benefits it is important to note that, whereas costs of loss prevention are fairly certain and definite, the payback to loss prevention may itself be either fairly certain if the individual is fully insured, or highly uncertain and speculative if he is not. It is clear that decisions on loss prevention will depend on both the degree of uncertainty inherent in the schedule of costs and benefits and the individual's reaction to that uncertainty.

When the individual is fully insured, the optimal level of expenditure on loss prevention is that which maximises the surplus of the costs over the expected value of the benefits. Thus if $r$ is the cost of loss prevention and the expected benefit is $F(r)$ (this reads, the expected benefit $F$ is a function of, or depends upon, $r$) then the surplus $S$ is given by the following term:

$$S = F(r) - r$$

Using standard calculus techniques, the optimum can be found by equating the derivative of this term with zero. This gives:

$$\frac{dS}{dr} = F'(r) - 1 = 0$$

or

$$F'(r) = 1 \tag{2.1}$$

If the individual is not insured, then account must be taken of his attitude towards risk.[9] The general case is that he will maximise the surplus of the *utility* value of the reduction in the expected value of loss $U[E'(r)]$ over the *utility* value of the expenditure on loss prevention $U(r)$. This gives the maximising condition:

$$U'[E'(r)] = U'(r) \tag{2.2}$$

A special case of equation 2.2 arises when the individual is indifferent to risk; here the optimality conditions can be specified as:

$$E'(r) = 1 \tag{2.3}$$

*Rational expenditure on loss prevention under different premium structures*

Where insurance premiums are completely independent of the expected claims cost (these are labelled non-actuarial premiums) and the individual is fully insured, there is no incentive to instal safety devices. (This was shown in Fig. 2.1.) At the other extreme, the premium may be equated to the actuarial value of the risk, this being the expected claim cost or the 'pure premium'. An insurer charging such a premium would find that, over a long period, claims payments and premium receipts would be in balance. The other implications of actuarial premiums are that differences in premium between different insureds will reflect differences in the expected claims cost and that changes in the expected claims cost for a given insured will be reflected by equivalent changes in the premium payable. Consequently, if the insured undertakes a programme of loss prevention, his expected benefit will be the same as if he were uninsured, i.e. the reduction in the expected value of loss. Rational behaviour from the insured will lead him to a loss prevention programme under which he equates the marginal cost of loss prevention with the marginal reduction in premium as in equation 2.1. However, since the reduction in premium $F(r)$ will equal the reduction in expected claims cost $E(r)$, then equation 2.2 can be substituted by equation 2.3.

This does not necessarily mean that actuarial premiums will lead to the same level of expenditure on loss prevention as in the no insurance situation. The maximising condition in the no insurance case is given by equation 2.2. which only degenerates into equation 2.3 if there is indifference to risk. It is not possible, even by assuming aversion to risk, to reach a general conclusion that more or less loss prevention will result from the purchase of insurance. The comparison of levels of loss prevention under self-insurance and full insurance under actuarial terms will depend upon the shape of the individual's utility function and the loss probabilities involved. This problem is developed further in the appendix.

The major defect of this model is that the provision of insurance is not without cost – premiums have to cover administrative expenses, selling expenses, contributions to reserve funds and insurers' profits. A more useful approach is to assume that insurance premiums include a loading to cover these factors but that the form of this loading is crucial in terms of the effects for loss prevention. It is further assumed that the insurers can and do correctly calculate the actuarial value of the risk and that the premium loading is built onto this value. This is a very strong assumption and will be relaxed in subsequent chapters. Three forms of loading are considered. First, a loading which is a percentage mark-up on the actuarial value. The widespread use of target loss ratios in insurance rating suggest that this method of rating may be prevalent.[10] Secondly, the loading may be a lump sum mark-up which is not related to the actuarial value. Thirdly, the loading may be some combination of the first two. These three forms are shown in Table 2.1 together with a premium which is equal to the expected

Table 2.1

Effect of a 50 per cent reduction in
expected claims cost under different premium structures

| Premium structure | | Premium | | Return to loss prevention programme |
| --- | --- | --- | --- | --- |
| | | Original risk | After loss prevention programme | |
| (1) Non-actuarial premium | $P = k$ | $k$ | $k$ | nil |
| (2) Actuarial premium | $P = E$ | $E$ | $E/2$ | $E/2$ |
| (3) Proportional loading | $P = (1 + m)E$ | $(1 + m)E$ | $(1 + m)E/2$ | $(1 + m)E/2$ |
| (4) Lump sum loading | $P = E + p$ | $E + p$ | $E/2 + p$ | $E/2$ |
| (5) Combination of (3) and (4) | $P = (1 + n)E + q$ | $(1 + n)E + q$ | $(1 + n)E/2 + q$ | $(1 + n)E/2$ |

where $P$ = premium;
$E$ = expected claims cost;
$k, m, n, p$ and $q$ are constants such that:[11] $k > o$
$$m \geqslant q > o$$
$$p \geqslant q > o.$$

claims cost (i.e. the actuarial premium) and a premium which is independent of the expected claims cost (i.e. the non-actuarial premium). The
effects of a loss prevention programme which reduces the expected claims
cost by 50 per cent are now compared under each of the premium structures.

The non-actuarial premium zero shows return to loss prevention and
this leads to the undiluted moral hazard argument illustrated in Fig. 2.1.
The actuarial premium allocates a return of premium equal to the full
expected reduction in claims costs. The lump sum loading has identical
effects to the actuarial premium whereas both the proportional loading
and the combination loading imply a return of premium in excess of the
reduction in expected claims costs.

The optimal loss prevention programme for the individual who is fully
insured is now illustrated in Fig. 2.3. This will be achieved, under the terms
of equation 2.1, where the marginal cost of loss prevention *HJ* is equated
to the marginal payback measured as a premium reduction. Under premium structure (1), the non-actuarial premium, the optimal level of
expenditure is that denoted by [1] on the horizontal axis. With (2) the
actuarial premium structure and (4) the lump sum loading the premium
reduction is equal to the reduction in the expected claims cost *PP* and the
optimal programme for the individual is denoted by the intersection of *PP*
and *HJ* at [2/4] on the horizontal axis. With (3), the proportionate pre-

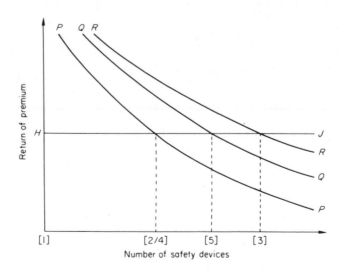

Fig. 2.3   The effect of premium incentives on loss prevention

mium loading, and (5), the combination loading, the returns of premium for loss prevention are denoted by $RR$ and $QQ$ respectively. These lead to loss prevention programmes of magnitudes [3] and [5] respectively. The appendix further develops the analysis of loss prevention under different premium structures.

## Socially optimal expenditure on loss prevention

From the viewpoint of society as a whole, the optimal level of expenditure on loss prevention is that which maximises the surplus of benefits over costs measured in terms of the *utilities* of those to whom the costs and benefits accrue. The use of utility values gives rise to serious problems in identifying the social optimum since valuations of costs and benefits will be personal and will vary according to where they fall. Without insurance, the costs and benefits are largely confined to the owner of the property and possibly third parties who may suffer from his actions. With insurance, they are distributed between the insured and third parties and the insurer who may well have differing attitudes towards risk. Consequently, the socially optimal level of loss prevention varies according to the distribution of insurance protection. It is convenient to avoid these problems of inter-personal comparison of utility and to identify the optimum at that level where the *money* value of expected benefits minus costs is maximised.

There is another reason why the optimum level of expenditure might depend upon the presence and level of insurance protection. Insurance redistributes the costs of hazards such as fire, injury, automobile collisions and the like and, in doing so, satisfies a consumer desire for security of future income. The social cost of these hazards therefore includes the costs of providing insurance services and, consequently, the social benefit of loss prevention includes any reduction in these costs. The socially optimal level of expenditure on loss prevention can therefore be defined (ignoring utility problems) as that level which equates marginal costs with the sum of the reduction in the expected value of losses and the reduction in the cost of resources consumed in underwriting these losses. Optimal incentives for loss prevention are provided when the premium reduction is equated with the sum of the reduction in claims cost and the consequent reduction in overhead costs. A premium structure which discriminates between good and bad risks in this manner will be labelled efficient.

As mentioned, insurers' costs may be divided roughly between claims costs, claims handling expenses, underwriting expenses, renewal expenses, and commission contributions to reserve funds and profits. Whilst some of

21

these items may be expected to be closely related to claims costs, particularly claims handling expenses, there is little information about whether the cost of providing other functions, e.g. renewal expenses, is at all related to claims. Underwriting expenses may bear some relationship to the expected claims cost but there are certain elements which might be considered as fixed costs, e.g. writing the policy, and filing and storage of records. It may even be that underwriting costs are more closely related to the value at risk rather than the expected value of claims.

Although there has been little empirical work on the determinants of insurers' overheads there is a *prima facie* case for suggesting that neither a lump sum loading nor a proportionate loading on premiums will achieve an efficient allocation of costs as between different risk groups. The former will provide an effective subsidy from good to bad risk insureds if at least some of the overhead cost is related to expected claims. The latter will result in an effective subsidy from bad to good risk insureds if at least some of the overhead cost is independent of expected claims. A simple and more efficient alternative would appear to be the combination loading discussed above, i.e. $P = (1 + n)E + q$ where the values of $n$ and $q$ are subject to empirical investigation and determination.[12]

If it is accepted that the most efficient form of premium structure incorporates a combination loading, then the socially optimal level of expenditure on loss prevention (ignore utilities) is higher when insurance is purchased than when no insurance is purchased. Insurance under conditions of lump sum loading will fall short of the optimum, even though this may be equal to or in excess of the actual level of expenditure under conditions of self insurance.

Finally, insurance under a proportionate loading structure will be expected to lead to socially excessive expenditures on loss prevention.

**Risk sharing**

Apart from premium concessions, another control by which the effects of moral hazard might be reduced is risk sharing. However, if moral hazard is to be offset in this way there is a corresponding social loss since the benefits of risk transfer are partially lost.[13] Under risk sharing arrangements such as co-insurance, deductible, franchise or first loss[14] the insured retains a financial stake in losses and consequently benefits directly from improvements in the risk. For example, in Fig. 2.1, the insured would install no safety devices if he was fully insured and if no premium return was forthcoming. Retaining a non-actuarial premium but limiting insurance to 50 per cent on a co-insurance basis, the net marginal benefit of safety devices to the insured would be $F'G'$ and he would maximise his expected return by installing $OX'$ safety devices.

Risk sharing may either be encouraged or imposed by the insurer or be requested by the insured. Thus small deductibles are commonly used, particularly in motor insurance, to eliminate small claims with disproportionately high claims experience. Other insurances, particularly liability, are often arranged on a first loss basis in order to stabilise underwriting experience by limiting payments for catastrophe losses.

The particular form of risk sharing may determine the type of loss prevention which may be adopted. Different risk sharing devices affect different parts of the insured's net loss distribution. For example, a deductible cuts off the right-hand side of the distribution by removing all possibility of financial loss to the insured above a particular amount. The distorting effects of insurance arranged on this basis are consequently to remove the incentive to limit the size of loss. Possibilities such as the subdivision of a fire risk into small independent risk units by the construction of party walls will not carry any personal pay-off to the insured but extra precautions to remove the smaller run of the mill losses may still prove financially attractive. At the other extreme, a first loss policy will retain the financial stake which the insured has in large losses but not in small ones. Accordingly, the insured may be more willing to undertake catastrophe planning than simple loss avoidance action.

Insurers sometimes specifically use deductibles or other forms of risk sharing to combat suspected moral hazard but normally only in situations where the moral hazard is of a character type. Whilst deductibles are fairly commonly used in certain branches of liability insurance to combat moral hazard, e.g. products liability and professional indemnity, and often in aviation insurance, their use for this purpose in property insurance is sporadic.[15] Also in motor insurance, whilst deductibles serve the dual purpose of limiting the number of small claims and reducing moral hazard, the fact that only small deductibles are usually imposed suggests that the first of these reasons is the dominant one. The attitude of insurers is conveniently summarised by G.L. Head: 'Historically, control of moral hazard was once advanced as a justification for not permitting full fire coverage . . . This belief, if it persists today, is seldom made explicit.'[16]

The initiative for risk sharing may alternatively come from the insured. There are strong theoretical reasons for suggesting that, under many premium structures, the optimal level of insurance is something less than full coverage. Thus it can be shown that where insurances include a proportionate loading of the form discussed above it is always optimal for the insured to self-insure some part of his risk, be it as a deductible or as co-insurance. It is only where there is a lump sum loading that risk sharing becomes suboptimal.[17] These theoretical conclusions may be of limited value since they do not include relevant features such as the effects of taxation on premiums and uninsured losses and alternative strategies such as the financing of losses by funding or external borrowing. However, it has been shown that in considering these features the insured might well benefit by undertaking part of the risk himself, though the optimal result depends very much on individual circumstance.[18]

Whilst these somewhat formal and mathematical models may rarely be used to devise strategy by insurance buyers, the good sense of their conclusions is reflected in actual practice. Thus in one survey in the United States it was revealed that 83 per cent of the top 500 industrial firms and 61 per cent of the second 500 practised some self-insurance. Of the top 500, 14 per cent retained more than 25 per cent of their insurable risk.[19] A survey of insurance managers in the United Kingdom shows a more modest level of self-insurance with less than 13 per cent practising some self-insurance on fire risk and, at the other extreme, nearly 72 per cent self-insuring on their credit risk.[20] However, the size of the retained risk is not revealed.

The underlying philosophy of risk management is that the individual will identify and evaluate risk and then adopt comprehensive strategy to deal with those risks. The available tools include the transfer of risk, the retention of risk and the reduction/prevention of risk. Since these may be interdependent the optimal strategy will probably involve a combination of the various tools. The particularly interesting thing about the spread of risk management is that it signifies a more systematic approach to risk and correspondingly strengthens the assumption of the rational approach of this and the next chapter.

## Notes

[1] The presentation follows R. Turvey, 'On divergences between cost and private cost', *Economica*, August 1963, p.30.

[2] R.M. Coase, 'The problem of social cost', *Journal of Law and Economics*, October 1960, p.3.

[3] J.M. Buchannan, *The Inconsistencies of the National Health Service*, Institute of Economic Affairs Occasional Paper 7, London 1964.

[4] M.V. Pauly, 'The economics of moral hazard comment', *American Economic Review*, June 1968, 58, p.535.

[5]  M.V. Pauly, op.cit.

[6]  See R.I. Mehr and E. Cammack, *Principles of Insurance*, 4th ed, R.D. Irwin, Homewood, 1966, pp.22–3. See also C. Arthur Williams and R.M. Heins, *Risk Management and Insurance*. McGraw Hill 1964, p.51, for a similar distinction.

[7]  See *Castellain v Preston* (1883), 11 QBD, 380 C.A.

[8]  It is arguable whether policies subject to replacement value clauses, or the new range of household policies which assess payment on the basis of the cost of replacement with a new item are contracts of indemnity. Whilst in some cases they permit financial gain by the insured, it is not clear whether there is pecuniary gain where the insured has available only limited options – replacement with a new item *or* perhaps non-replacement of the destroyed item. This situation arises for goods for which there is no well developed secondhand market and where replacement must satisfy new regulations which were not in force at the time of the original purchase, e.g. new planning regulations for factory buildings.

[9]  Two cases arise, aversion to risk and love of risk. A risk averter is one for whom dispersion in the range of possible future outcomes is an undesirable quality; the greater the dispersion the less desirable the prospect. Conversely, for the risk lover dispersion is a desirable quality. Thus given a choice between two alternatives having the same actuarial value but the one having less dispersion than the other (e.g. self-insurance *or* insurance at an actuarially fair premium), the risk averter would choose the alternative with the lower dispersion (insurance) whereas the risk lover would opt for the other alternative (self-insurance). The risk averter will be willing to forego income to reduce dispersion in the range of possible future outcomes whereas the risk lover needs to be compensated in order to accept a less risky future.

[10]  Insurers use target loss ratios to set premium rates for classes of business. Premiums for a class of insureds are fixed at a level which will achieve some desired proportional relationship to expected claims cost. If the premium structure fully reflects differences in actuarial value between risks within the class then this practice implies a proportionate loading for individual risks.

[11]  The conditions $m \geqslant n$ and $p \geqslant q$ are imposed to focus on the *form* of the mark-up rather than its *level*. The latter will be largely determined by competitive conditions.

[12]  Alternative forms might also be considered which relate overhead costs to the sum insured.

[13]  R. Zeckhauser, 'A case study of the tradeoff between risk spreading

and appropriate incentives', *Journal of Economic Theory*, 2, 10–26 (1970).

[14] With co-insurance the insurers only underwrite a percentage of the risk, the rest being retained by the insured. With deductibles (excesses) the insurers limit their liability to the difference between the amount of the loss and a fixed sum. With a franchise the insurers are only liable for losses above a fixed sum. Under first loss policies the insurers define an upper limit to their liability.

[15] See *Sigma*, 1 January 1974, pp.10–11.

[16] G.L. Head, *Insurance to Value*, S.S. Hebner Foundation, R.D. Irwin, Homewood 1971, p.164.

[17] See J. Mossin, 'Aspects of rational insurance purchasing', *Journal of Political Economy*, vol.76, 1968; V.L. Smith, 'Optimal insurance coverage', *Journal of Political Economy*, vol.76, 1968; N.A. Doherty, 'Some fundamental theorems of risk management', *Journal of Risk and Insurance*, vol.43, no.3, September 1975.

[18] See A.E. Hofflander, E. Renshaw and V. Renshaw, 'Optimal insurance', *Journal of Risk and Insurance*, vol.38, no.2, June 1971; and M.H. Atkins, N.A. Doherty and R.L. Carter, 'Risk insurance and the growing firm', University of Nottingham Discussion Papers in Industrial Economics, no.2, 1975.

[19] 'Survey on corporate attitudes towards property and liability insurers', *Fortune Magazine,* 1974.

[20] 'The status and techniques of insurance managers in industry and commerce', Association of Insurance Managers in Industry and Commerce, London 1972.


APPENDIX

A formal presentation of the interdependency between insurance and loss prevention is shown by considering the effects of an exogenous change in the level of insurance on the optimality conditions for loss prevention. This procedure will reveal that insurance and loss prevention are substitutes (i.e. an increase in insurance protection will lead to a reduction in the demand for loss prevention) or complements (an increase in insurance protection will cause expenditure on loss prevention to increase). For simplicity, the risk is assumed to be shared on a co-insurance basis. The individual will wish to maximise the expected utility which is represented by:[1]

$$U = (1 - p(r))U(A - a L \pi(r) - r + p(r)U(A - a L\pi (r) -(1 - a)L - r)$$

$$(2A.1)$$

where $p$ is the probability of loss;

$\quad$ $r$ is the level of expenditure on loss prevention;

$\quad$ $A$ is the initial level of the insured's wealth;

$\quad$ $a$ is the percentage of the risk insured;

$\quad$ $L$ is the size of the loss; and

$\quad$ $\pi$ is the premium payable.

The optimal level of loss prevention for any given level of insurance is given by the first order condition:

$$\frac{\partial U}{\partial r} = -p'(r) \left\{ U(A - a\pi (r)L - r) - U(A - a\pi (r)L - (1 -a)L - r) \right\}$$
$$-(1 - p(r))U_1' (a \pi ' (r)L + 1) - p(r)U_0' (a \pi ' (r)L + 1) = 0$$

$$(2A.2)$$

In order to show how the optimal level of loss prevention changes with changes in the level of insurance, the derivative of the first order condition is taken to give $Nda + Mdr = 0$ or $dr/da = -N/M$. Here $M$ is the second order condition which, since equation (2A.1) is to be maximised, will be negative. Therefore the sign of $dr/da$ will be the same as that of $N$. $N$ is given by:

$$N = p'(r) \left\{ U_1' L \pi(r) - U_0' L (\pi(r) - 1) \right\}$$

$$-(1 - p(r))U_1' L \pi ' (r) + (1 - p(r))U_1'' (aL \pi ' (r) + 1)L \pi (r)$$

$$-p(r)U_0' L \pi ' (r) + p(r)U_0'' (aL \pi ' (r) + 1) (L(\pi (r) - 1)) \quad (2A.3)$$

*Actuarial premium* With the premium equal to the actuarial value of the risk, $\pi(r) = p(r)$ and $N$ simplifies to:

$$Lp'(r) (2p(r) - 1) (U_1' - U_0') + L(a Lp(r) + 1)p(r) (1 - p(r)) (U_1'' - U_0'')$$

$$(2A.4)$$

This expression may be either positive or negative; thus insurance and loss prevention may be either complements or substitutes. It can be shown that if $p$ is not very small and $U$ is concave, then complementarity would ensue.[2, 3]

*Lump sum loading* If the premium is of the form $aLp(r) + k$ then equation (2A.3) would simplify in exactly the same way as equation

(2A.4) and, since $M$ would also be unchanged, the result is the same as the actuarial case.

*Proportionate loading*   When a proportionate loading of the form $\pi(r) = (1 + m)p(r)$ (where $m > 1$,) is substituted into equation (2A.1), $N$ becomes:

$$p'(r)L \left\{ (2p(r) (1 + m) - 1) (U_1' - U_0') - mU_1' \right\}$$

$$+ L(a\,L(1 + m)p'(r) + 1) \left\{ p(r) (1 - p(r) - mp(r)) (U_1'' - U_0'') + mp(r)U_1'' \right\}$$

$$(2A.5)$$

The conditions for a positive sign for this expression are more complex. For example, if $U$ is quadratic, then $N$ will certainly be positive if:

$$(2p(r) (1 + m) - 1) > 0$$

*and*

$$\frac{U_1''}{U_1'} < \frac{p'(r)}{p(r) (aL(1 + m)p'(r) + 1)}$$

and may be positive if only one of these conditions is met. Furthermore, complementarity is likely to occur at lower levels of $p$ under a proportionate loading than in the actuarial or lump sum cases. It may also be noted that the lower the coefficient of risk aversion, the more likely it is that insurance and loss prevention will turn out to be complementary. In the limit, $dr/da$ will certainly be positive if $U$ is linear since the firm will maximise its expected return.

*Combination loading*   With a combination loading of the form $\pi(r) = (1 + n)p(r) + k$ then the result turns out to be of the same form as equation (2A.5) and the same general conclusion holds. However, as mentioned in the text, if $n < m$, then the level of loss prevention under this premium structure will turn out to be less than under the proportionate loading.

**Notes**

[1]  The methodology follows that in N.A. Doherty, 'Some fundamental theorems of risk management', *Journal of Risk and Insurance*, vol.43, no.3, September 1975.

[2]  I. Ehrlich and G.S. Becker, 'Market insurance, self insurance and self protection', *Journal of Political Economy*, vol.80, 1972.

[3]  Note that $(aLp'(r) + 1)$ is positive by the first order condition.

# 3 Rational models of insurer behaviour

The purpose of chapter 2 was to show that the value of loss prevention to the insured depended on the availability and conditions of insurance protection. The relationships which emerged depended on the incentives which the insurers built into the insurance contract and, in particular, the degree to which the premium structure discriminated between different insureds according to the costs they each impose on the insurance fund. In order to provide a discriminatory premium structure, the insurer must have information on the factors which determine the probability and/or severity of loss. Thus changes in these factors may be rewarded or penalised by premium adjustments. But the assembly of such information is not costless nor does it have neutral implications for the profitability of insurance operations. This chapter examines the effects of the spread of loss prevention on the market demand and cost curves of insurers and the part played by market mechanisms in inducing insurers to: (a) undertake a search for information on loss probabilities and loss prevention; (b) monitor the insured's spending on loss prevention; and (c) embody this information in a discriminatory rating structure. The following chapter examines the effectiveness of different types of premium structures in disseminating information on the efficiency of different loss prevention devices.

## Loss prevention and insurer profitability

Let us suppose that an individual's demand for insurance depends upon three factors: (a) the price of insurance; (b) the expected value of losses; and (c) some measure of dispersion of his probability distribution over future losses which will indicate the degree of uncertainty surrounding future events. Since the function of insurance is to transfer risk, the insured exchanges certain present income for future uncertain income. The price of insurance might therefore be considered as the rate at which this exchange takes place and will be expressed in such terms as $x$ pence per £$y$ of cover. An individual may vary the amount of cover by co-insurance or

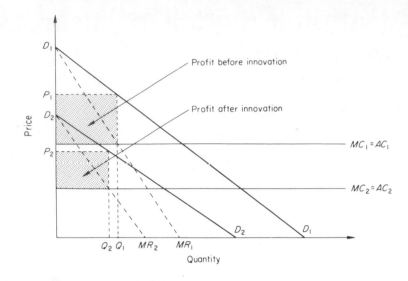

Fig. 3.1    The effect of innovation on insurer profitability

some other form of risk sharing. If the market demand for insurance is considered, changes in demand might also occur if greater or fewer individuals buy insurance.

The effect of loss prevention will be to reduce the expected value of losses for the individuals concerned and will probably also affect the dispersion in their probability distributions. Such innovations will tend to shift the industry cost curve of insurers downwards from $C_1$ to $C_2$ as shown in Fig. 3.1. The marginal cost curves are shown and are assumed constant merely for simplification. In addition, an interdependence between the demand for insurance and the expected value of losses has already been noted and consequently loss prevention may be expected to shift the market demand curve. At any given price the insured would purchase less insurance and/or fewer insureds would purchase any insurance. Consequently the market demand curve (or revenue curve) would shift inwards towards the origin from $D_1$ to $D_2$.

The implications of innovations in loss prevention on the profitability of insurance operations will depend largely upon two factors: first, the relationship between the shifts in the cost and demand curves, and, secondly, the pricing strategy adopted by the insurer.

The marginal revenue curves before and after loss prevention are shown in Fig. 3.1 as $MR_1$ and $MR_2$ respectively. If the collective profit of the industry is to be maximised by a single price/output decision (e.g. if there is

30

a monopolist insurer or if insurers form a cartel), then the price/output decision will be determined at the intersection of the marginal cost and revenue curves. This gives the price/output combinations $P_1 Q_1$ and $P_2 Q_2$ before and after loss prevention. The effect on profit is indicated by comparison of the two shaded areas. Loss prevention may increase or reduce the collective profit of insurers; the result depends on the interaction of the cost and demand curves and no general comment can be made here.

This discussion gives rise to the following policy issues.

(1)    The collective benefits for insurers from the spread of loss prevention are ambiguous. It may increase or reduce profitability. The promotion of loss prevention research and the provision of information and propaganda on loss prevention will only be favourable to insurers if it reacts on cost curves more intensively than on demand curves.

(2)    There may also be less direct benefits from the active promotion of loss prevention, particularly in the field of improved relations with the public and government.

Whatever the collective advantages/disadvantages to insurers of loss prevention, the effects which insurance has on loss prevention will largely be determined by the pricing strategies of individual insurers and, in particular, the extent to which these strategies discriminate between good and bad risks.

## Models of premium rating — the profit maximising insurer

### The discriminating monopolist

The starting point for a model of discriminatory rating is to consider the behaviour of a monopolist insurer whose objective is to maximise profits. The monopolist may be represented by a single insurer or a cartel under which price deviations between insurers are excluded by agreement. The insurer has a portfolio of insureds who may be divided into two subgroups. In the first subgroup the expected claims cost for each policy is £x whereas the expected claims cost for each policy in the second subgroup is £y, where £y > £x. These subgroups are labelled good risks and bad risks respectively and, for the time being, it is assumed that insureds within each subgroup are identical.

If the insurer is unable to distinguish between good and bad risks, he may consider his optimal policy to be to adopt a single price which is

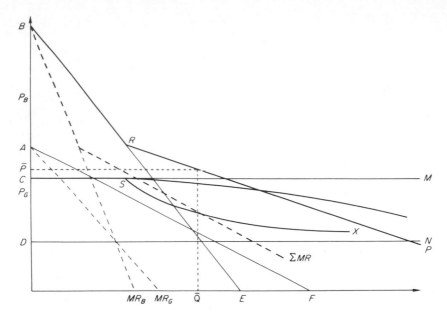

Fig. 3.2    Profit maximising rating strategy

payable by all insureds and which equates aggregate marginal cost with aggregate marginal revenue. This policy is illustrated in Fig. 3.2. The demand curve for good risks is shown as $AF$ and $BE$ is the demand curve for bad risks. The aggregate demand curve facing the insurer is given by horizontal summation as $BRP$. The marginal revenue curves are constructed in dotted lines and are labelled $MR_G$, $MR_B$ and $\Sigma MR$ for good risks, bad risks and total portfolio respectively. The marginal cost curves for the bad and good risk groups are shown as $CM$ and $DN$ respectively; constant marginal costs are assumed only to simplify the diagrams. The aggregate marginal cost curve for the whole portfolio is shown as $CSX$.[1] It may be noted that each cost curve embraces both claims costs and other underwriting expenses such as administrative costs, contributions to reserves and commission.

The single profit maximising price for the insurer who is unable to distinguish between good and bad risks is given by equating aggregate marginal revenue $\Sigma MR$ and aggregate marginal cost $CSX$. This gives a price of $\overline{P}$ and a quantity of $\overline{Q}$.

The standard economic model of a discriminating monopolist reveals that, when it is possible to separate demand into several markets, the optimal (profit maximising) policy is to charge different prices to different

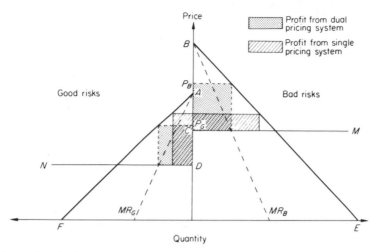

Fig. 3.3   Discriminatory rating strategy – normal case

customers.[2] Effective separation of markets requires that the 'consumer cannot resell the product to another'.[3] This assumption of non-transferability of the product is normally met with insurance contracts which are usually specific with respect to the person and the subject matter insured. It therefore becomes a straightforward task to adapt this model to the insurance situation to produce a theory of discriminatory insurance rating.

Referring again to Fig. 3.2, the insurer is able to increase his profits by rejecting the single price $\overline{P}$ applicable to both good and bad risks and, in its place, substituting a dual pricing system. Good risks are charged price $P_G$ which equates the marginal cost and marginal revenue for good risks; similarly, bad risks are charged a different price, namely $P_B$. The effect on profitability is shown in Fig. 3.3 which separates the good and bad risk markets into separate quadrants. The labelling of curves follows Fig. 3.2 and the profitability of the non-discriminatory and discriminatory pricing strategies can be compared by the shaded profit areas. If the assumption of homogeneity of risks within risk subgroups is dropped, then profit maximising strategy might ultimately involve a different price for each insured.[4] However, if information is not costless, this process of subdivision and refinement of rating categories will be constrained at a point where the marginal costs of information outweigh the benefits of further subdivision.[5]

It is now necessary to examine whether the price discrimination brought about under monopolistic conditions is likely to produce an efficient set of incentives for expenditure on loss prevention. Profit is defined as the surplus of total revenue over total costs and this is shown separately for the good and bad risk markets:

$$\pi_G = P_G Q_G - C_G(Q_G) \quad \text{and} \quad \pi_B = P_B Q_B - C_B(Q_B) \qquad (3.1)$$

where $\pi$ is profit, $P$ is price, $Q$ is quantity, $PQ$ is total revenue and $C(Q)$ is total cost. Subscripts $G$ and $B$ refer to good and bad risks.

Profit for the insurer will be maximised by choosing those separate prices which maximise each of the functions. This can be shown using calculus techniques by equating the partial derivatives with zero to give the following conditions:

$$\frac{d\pi_G}{dQ_G} = \left[ P_G + \frac{dP_G}{dQ_G} Q_G \right] - \left[ \frac{dC_G}{dQ_G} \right] = 0 \qquad (3.2a)$$

and

$$\frac{d\pi_B}{dQ_B} = \left[ P_B + \frac{dP_B}{dQ_B} Q_B \right] - \left[ \frac{dC_B}{dQ_B} \right] = 0 \qquad (3.2b)$$

The term in the first bracket in each of these equations is simply the marginal revenue and the term in the second bracket is the marginal cost. These terms can now be re-arranged as follows:

$$P_B - P_G = \left[ \frac{dC_B}{dQ_B} - \frac{dC_G}{dQ_G} \right] - \left[ \frac{dP_B}{dQ_B} Q_B - \frac{dP_G}{dQ_G} Q_G \right] \qquad (3.3)$$

This expression shows the difference in premium between a good risk insured and a bad risk insured or, alternatively, the return of premium for an insured who has reduced the expected value of his claims and can now be reclassified from a bad to a good risk. The first bracket on the right hand side of the equation shows the difference in marginal costs to the insurer of underwriting a bad risk as against a good risk. It includes both claims costs and other costs. If overhead costs such as underwriting and selling expenses do not vary between good and bad risks then the first term will equal the expected reduction in claims costs if one insured is transformed from a bad to a good risk. The presence of the second bracket reflects the monopolist's ability to recoup economic rent. This term may be positive or negative depending on the shape and position of the respective demand curves of good and bad risk insureds.

34

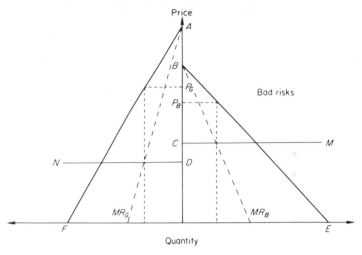

Fig. 3.4   Discriminatory rating strategy – adverse incentives

It is conceivable, given this analysis, that an insured undertaking a programme of loss prevention would be rewarded for his troubles with a demand for a higher premium. This is illustrated in Fig. 3.4 which is similar in presentation and labelling to Fig. 3.3 except that the demand curve for good risks has been shifted outwards. This curious result could occur if the loss prevention programme undertaken by an individual coincided with a sudden and large revision in his attitude towards risks. Casual empiricism suggests that a situation of higher prices for better risks is unlikely to prevail in the real world and a more plausible hypothesis is that the quantity of insurance demanded at any given price is, under *ceteris paribus* assumptions, positively related to the expected value of losses.[6] This alternative hypothesis suggests non-negative premium discounts for loss prevention as indicated by Figs. 3.2 and 3.3.

Summarising, a monopolist insurer may be able to attain satisfactory levels of profit without operating a pricing structure which discriminates between good and bad risks. However, a profit maximising strategy would involve some form of price discrimination between different risk groups but premium differences will not necessarily reflect differences in the costs of underwriting insureds from the respective risk groups.

*Competition and insurance pricing*

The introduction of competition into this model will have two effects: first, there will be intensified pressure for insurers to operate discriminatory

35

rating structures and secondly, the distortions in premium incentives for loss prevention due to the exploitation of monopoly rent will, in the case of intensive competition, be removed. The first of these effects has been described quite simply in the following terms. 'If one company charges a premium of £20 over a group of cars which could be broken down into two groups at £15 and £25, another company will spot this differential, offer a premium of £15.10s. [£15·50] for the "£15" group and take the business at a profit while the original company is left with the "£25" business at the £20 rate and a fast deteriorating experience.'[7] This process, where choices made by insureds leave concentrations of bad (or good) risks in the portfolios of certain insurers, is called 'selection'.

The process of selection is now described in more detail. The starting point is with a market controlled by one insurer (insurer 1) who under-writes good and bad risks at a single premium. A new entrant to the market (insurer 2) notices that the portfolio can be divided between the good and bad risks and offers a lower premium, accepting only the good risks. There are two effects on insurer 1: first, his demand function will be shifting; secondly, since its composition between good and bad risks will be chang-ing, so too will his cost functions. At the original price, insurer 1 will sell less good risk policies at the given price, but the effect of increased competition will be to make his demand curve more elastic. This is shown in Fig. 3.5 as the new demand curve $B R' P'$. Similarly, insurer 1's marginal cost function will change from $C$ to $C'$.

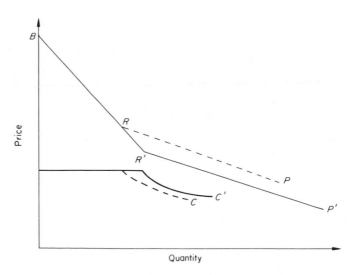

Fig. 3.5   The effects of competition on the insurer's demand curve

Several outcomes are possible. First of all, insurer 1 may still not spot the differential between good and bad risks and may continue to charge a single price. In the case illustrated in Fig. 3.5 his second best strategy could either involve a lower price, in which case he would win back some of the good risks but enhance his losses on the bad risk business, or raising the price, which would accentuate the movement of good risks out of the portfolio but would also reduce the subsidy to bad risk business. Either way, if competition for good risk insureds is severe, then in the long term he will be unable to compete in this market at a price sufficient to cover the costs of his combined good and bad risk portfolio and he will therefore be forced out of business altogether or be forced to raise his price and operate solely in the bad risk market.

The alternative possibility is that, in view of the combination of declining demand and increasing costs, insurer 1 may re-examine his portfolio, spot the heterogeneity and devise a rating structure which discriminates between good and bad risk insureds. Thus the general effect of competition, which is based on access to information concerning cost differentials for different insureds, will be to promote one of the following market structures, or perhaps some mixture of the two:

(1)   A market in which each insurer operates a premium structure which discriminates between good and bad risks; or
(2)   A market in which each insurer specialises in either good risks or bad risks.

In each case the logic of the argument allows for further subdivision into finer risk categories simply by dropping the assumption that insureds within each of the subgroups are identical. Furthermore, under either market structure, an insured can secure a reduction in his insurance premium by undertaking a programme of loss prevention which transforms his risk from a bad to a good risk: the principal difference is that under market structure (1) he need not change his insurer to obtain such a discount, but under market structure (2) he has to shop around.

The implications for efficient premium discrimination depend upon the intensity of competition. In the extreme case, competition may be so severe as to remove any surplus profit made by insurers. Insurers will face a highly elastic demand curve and a competitive solution may be reached at which the price is equal to the marginal cost. This solution will be reached under perfect or highly intensive competition: the dominant feature is that the individual insurer is a price taker. With price equated to marginal cost for each risk group, the differences in price between two risk groups, and consequently the payback to loss prevention, is clearly the difference in the marginal cost between the good and bad risk groups. Under the analysis of chapter 2 this premium structure can be said to provide an efficient set of incentives for loss prevention.

Between the two extremes of monopoly and perfect competition economic theory has identified a range of intermediate solutions. Under monopolistic competition there is a large number of producers but a degree of product differentiation allows individual producers a certain amount of monopoly profit. The oligopoly model describes a market of few sellers but with a high degree of interdependence between their business strategies. The degree of interdependence in insurance markets and the relatively high levels of concentration suggest that this model may be the most pertinent but, unfortunately, it is this model for which economic theory has produced the most ambiguous conclusions. The pricing strategies adopted by firms depend on whether they anticipate the counter-reactions of rival firms to any changes in their own prices. These conditions have led to the opposing predictions of price warfare and price stability. In addition, the interdependence and uncertainty of the oligopoly situation have also led to models of tacit or open collusion between producers. The size and strength of cartels are predominant features of insurance markets in Western Europe and North America and chapters 5 and 6 consider examples of their pricing behaviour.

## Other models of premium rating

In the model described, the insurer is assumed to be a profit maximiser: no other objectives are taken into account. Whilst it may be unrealistic to remove the profit objective for private insurers, it would be equally unrealistic to ignore competing objectives such as the level of sales, the conditions of employment and long term survival. These conflicts are acknowledged in a satisficing approach. Insurers may only seek to trade profit against other objectives up to a certain point. Insurers are content to achieve a satisfactory level of profits.

One suggestion is that firms, be it the owners, the managers or the employees, simply wish for a 'quiet life'. A vigorous pursuit of profit may involve the pressures of the 'rat race', may court the threat of government intervention, and may also evoke retaliatory action from competing firms which results in a price war. Clearly, some of these effects would threaten the long term survival of the company.

The dangers of unbridled competition have certainly been realised by insurers and is evidenced by the widespread formation of cartels for rate making. Even though some cartels may be explicitly committed to discriminatory rating, the underlying agreement amongst members to support a system of fixed or minimum prices excludes the form of selective competition outlined in this chapter. On the other hand, cartel rating is usually based upon a central pool of data which provides a larger and more reliable statistical sample than that available to the individual company. Examples of such cartels and their implications for discriminatory rating are considered in chapters 5 and 6.

The profit maximising model rests on marginal adjustments between cost and revenue to achieve an optimal price output combination. An alternative approach which dovetails more neatly with satisficing objective is a cost plus model of pricing. Under this model, the producer charges a price sufficient to cover his costs and allow a margin for profit. There is strong evidence to suggest that insurers do fix prices in this way. Thus one writer notes that: '. . . the general assumption is that insurers fix their premium rates in relation to expected claims costs adding an allowance for expenses and profit',[8] and another: 'But what evidence we have suggests that in both life and general insurance the insurers adopt uniform cost-plus pricing policies and do not attempt to fix premiums in relation to marginal costs'.[9] In its naive form, with the mark-up for expenses and profit pitched at a constant percentage over all classes of risk, the cost plus hypothesis suggests that insurers' profits are directly related to the expected claims costs. Consequently, as expected claims costs fall so too will profits. This clearly indicates that insurers acting from self-interest would discourage loss prevention and actively pursue bad risks for inclusion in their portfolio. This prediction is clearly at variance with actual practice. Nor does the model give any explanation of why insurers subdivide their portfolio into different risk groups and charge correspondingly different rates of premium.

The problem with this naive version of the cost plus hypothesis is that it ignores demand. It contains no suggestion as to how insurers calculate the mark-up or how it may be adjusted over time. If insurers take account of demand,[10] then the mark-up for expenses and profit might be considered as adjustable in the light of advice from marketing personnel. This version of the cost plus hypothesis is not incompatible with the profit maximising approach and the calculation and adjustment of the mark-up may be little more than a trial and error approach to the maximising solution.

One important point highlighted by the cost plus hypothesis is the widespread use of a proportionate loading. Thus it is common practice to subdivide a portfolio into appropriate risk groups on the basis of calculated or assumed differences in expected claims costs and then simply to add on to all these basic premiums a constant proportionate loading. Thus, whilst the loading may vary between different years according to changes in demand, it does not normally differ between different risk groups according to their respective demand.

The main profit maximising model developed in this chapter can be illustrated in a negative sense by examining the provision of insurance by the public sector. State insurance operates on a very different basis to that in the private sector and its most distinctive feature is the general absence of premium discrimination. This may be attributed to the differing objectives of the private and public sectors and to the absence of those market constraints which face the private sector. We are left with a situation in which the exception illustrates the rule.

The main areas in which the State acts explicitly as an underwriter lie in the provision of health insurance and in national insurance such as sickness, unemployment and industrial injury benefits. In each of these areas the prospect of a claim arising for a given individual will depend upon a variety of factors, many of which can be identified and measured. With health insurance and sickness insurance the probability of a claim and its probable magnitude will depend *inter alia* upon the age, medical history and occupation of the insured person. With unemployment benefit it will largely be determined by age, occupation, education, qualifications, previous employment history and geographical location of the insured person. The prospect of an industrial injury claim will rest largely upon age and the nature of occupation. The interaction of these various factors in explaining or predicting loss probabilities presents no greater technical difficulties than those which face private underwriters. Health insurance is underwritten in the private sector and employers' liability insurers face almost identical technical problems in measuring risk to those presented in industrial injury insurance. In spite of these comparisons, however, the financial system for state benefits is almost entirely non-discriminatory.

The sources of finance for the National Health and National Insurance systems comprises a set of contributions from employers and employees and the direct allocation of tax revenue from the Exchequer. The incidence of taxation bears no direct relationship to the distribution of benefits. Contributions, like direct taxation, are directly related to income. This bears at least some relationship to the distribution of benefits insofar as the National Insurance benefits include a limited supplement to the basic rate which is determined by the level of earnings. However, the burden of the contributions scale does not reflect the actuarial value of the earnings related supplement which might be paid. Apart from the earnings adjustment, the contributions operate at a flat rate with no variation according to the various causal or associated factors identified in the previous paragraph. In at least one case there was an abortive attempt to introduce a limited degree of premium discrimination into the contributions system. The Beveridge Report,[11] upon which the National Insurance system was founded, recommended that the industrial injuries scheme be financed by contributions from the employer, the employee and the State, but with a special levy on industries with a particularly bad accident record.[12] The proposal for a special levy was rejected by the government largely in the face of union opposition and the scheme in operation therefore does not differentiate contributions according to the degree of risk.

The absence of discriminatory rating may be attributed to the lack of competitive pressure on the state insurer. In part this reflects the unsuitability of the type of business undertaken by the State for private insurers (particularly unemployment insurance) but, more importantly, the Department of Health and Social Security can levy compulsory contributions. This explanation is insufficient in itself to cover the absence of premium discrimination since the monopoly model predicts a limited degree of discrimination for profit reasons. A more potent explanation of the lack of discrimination lies with the differing objectives of the public and private sectors.

When private insurers refer to equitable premiums they refer to discrimination between insureds according to the costs each imposes upon the insurance fund. In stating that equitable premiums are a policy objective they may simply be supporting their profit goal. For the state insurer the notion of equity might well become entangled with wider government objectives. In particular, the government may wish to influence the distribution of income and this objective may appear in two forms. First, the system of income related contributions may be set alongside the progressive fiscal system as a means of re-distributing income from rich to poor. Secondly, the absence of risk discrimination in the contribution redistributes income from high risk to low risk individuals. For some of the benefits, such as health and unemployment insurance, the actuarial premium which would be appropriate for some high risk individuals would be so high that it could not be met from the individual's current income or could only be met at the expense of basic necessities. This raises a direct choice between the denial of benefits to those unable to pay the appropriate premium or the operation of a system of subsidisation within the contributions structure. In the United Kingdom the government has chosen the second of these options in common with most other governments

41

of advanced industrialised economies.

An alternative role of government is achieved with the regulation of a private insurance sector. Whereas in the United Kingdom the government has concentrated its attention upon the adequacy of reserve funds, and more recently on the establishment of a guarantee fund to underwrite the failures of private insurers, the pattern of intervention in the United States has generally included direct control over rating. The general objective of rating regulation has been to steer a middle path such that rates are neither so low that insurer insolvency is threatened nor so high that excess profits are reaped, and, in addition, rates should be not 'unfairly discriminatory'.[13] 'Unfair price discrimination exists when there are price differences which do not correspond to differences in cost or cost differences which are not reflected in price differences'.[14] However, whilst a fairly discriminatory pricing system is envisaged in public policy objectives, the method of regulation, which has required the filing and approval of rates, has tended to discourage competitive mechanisms as described in chapter 4. The subject is raised again in chapter 5 but at this juncture it is worth noting that a new generation of state regulatory laws, the so-called 'open competition' rating laws, are attempting to harness the benefits of competition in the hope of attaining more efficient rating structures.[15]

Government regulation of the economy of a more general nature might disturb the relationship between insurance and loss prevention. For example, the operation of a freeze on prices may prevent insurers adjusting the loadings on bad risk business and so maintaining an appropriate differential between good and bad risks. Furthermore, the upwards inflexibility of prices may also explain why insurers wish to promote propaganda/information campaigns aimed at shifting cost curves.

The interdependence between insurance and loss prevention acts in both directions. Loss prevention will undermine the demand for insurance but, since it also reduces insurer's cost curves, the effects on insurer profitability are ambiguous. On the other hand, insurers, following their optimal pricing strategies, will devise premium structures which contain incentives for insureds to undertake loss prevention.

The ways in which insurers have promoted loss prevention activities follows a similar division: first, in terms of non-financial methods which are aimed generally at all insureds and, secondly, by financial inducement directed at specific insureds. The non-financial methods include the promotion of research on loss prevention, the dissemination of information, salvage operations, and propaganda such as advertisements, safety courses and safety competitions. It is unlikely that these activities consume a large volume of resources. Thus, for example, in UK fire insurance most

of these activities are undertaken by insurers acting in concert by supporting organisations such as the Joint Fire Research Organisation, the Fire
Protection Association, the Central Fire Liaison Panel and the Liverpool
and Glasgow Salvage Corps. The percentage of premium income allocated
by British Insurance Association members for these purposes is about
one-third of one per cent.[16] For employee safety, however, much of the
effort is on an individual basis by large specialist insurers and their
activities include the promotion of safety manuals and safety competitions.
In both these cases the loss prevention activity is incidental to the provision
of insurance services. This may be contrasted with the activities of
engineering insurers or the Factory Mutual System where insurance and
loss prevention represent a horizontal diversification of their activities and
loss of insurance business brought about by loss prevention may be made
good by their increased activities in the provision of loss prevention
services.

The financial inducements to loss prevention may turn out to be more
important, though their value depends on the ability of insurance premiums to convey accurate information on loss prevention systems. This
will be discussed in the next chapter.

## Notes

[1] The marginal cost curve for the whole portfolio is given by the
equation:

$$MC = \frac{\delta Q_G}{\delta Q} MC_G + \frac{\delta Q_B}{\delta Q} MC_B$$

where $Q$ is the aggregate quantity demanded, $Q_G$ and $Q_B$ are the quantities
demanded by the good and bad risks respectively, and $MC_G/MC_B$ are the
respective marginal cost curves.

[2] See, for example, K.J. Cohen and R.M. Cyert, *Theory of the Firm*,
Prentice Hall, Englewood Cliffs 1965, and other basic texts on pricing and
resource allocation.

[3] Cohen and Cyert, op.cit.

[4] This is called 'individual rating' and is described in chapter 4.

[5] See M.V. Pauly, 'Overinsurance and the public provision of insurance: the roles of moral hazard and adverse selection', *Quarterly Journal
of Economics,* February 1974.

[6] There is a danger here of confusing *differences* in demand between
(different) good and bad risk individuals and *changes* in demand when a

given individual changes his degree of risk. The discussion here refers to the latter.

[7] H.M. Scurfield, 'Motor insurance statistics', *Journal of the Institute of Actuaries Students Society,* vol.18, part 3, August 1968, p.208.

[8] R.L. Carter, *Economics and Insurance,* Policyholder Press, Stockport, 1973, p.136.

[9] G. Clayton, *British Insurance,* Elek Books, London 1971, p.306.

[10] See R.L. Carter, op.cit., p.138 and D.I.W. Reynolds, 'Motor insurance rate fixing', *Institute of Actuaries Students Society,* 1970.

[11] *Social Insurance and Allied Services,* report by Sir William Beveridge, HMSO, Cmd 6404, 1942.

[12] The Beveridge Report, op.cit., paras 86–9.

[13] See F.G. Crane, 'Insurance rate regulation: the reason why', *Journal of Risk and Insurance,* vol.39, 1972.

[14] C. Arthur Williams, *Price Discrimination in Property and Liability Insurance,* University of Minnesota Press, Minneapolis 1959, p.3.

[15] See D.R. Klock, 'Competitive rating laws and insurer conduct', *Journal of Risk and Insurance,* vol.39, 1972. In examining the Illinois Law he notes that it envisages that insurers will develop 'reasonable and equitable rate treatment for all insurance consumers'.

[16] Calculated from figures supplied by the British Insurance Association.

# 4 Information on loss prevention – the role of insurance pricing

The information problem is one of both scarcity and cost. If the insurer is to exercise the sort of price discrimination described in the last chapter he will require a detailed knowledge not only of his aggregate cost and revenue functions but also of how these are broken down between the different risk categories. Furthermore, if the insured is to act upon these incentives then it is important for social policy that premiums convey reliable information on underlying loss probabilities and changes in these probabilities resulting from the formation of loss prevention strategies. Information can be purchased by diverting resources from alternative usage into the construction of statistical and technical data. Since losses are random in their incidence, the most pertinent information on loss probabilities lies in the records of loss experience of comparable risks. Providing the risks are fundamentally similar and providing experience is not stretched out over periods of rapid technological and economic change, then the techniques of statistical inference may be used to estimate future loss probabilities. Appropriate rating structures can then be devised. Ideally, the role of insurers might be considered as a clearing house for information on the effectiveness of different forms of loss prevention. This information is then disseminated in the form of premium differentials which reflect the cost effectiveness of the different forms of loss prevention.

Whilst there are costs of collecting and assembling statistical information there are also other constraints on its use. The reliability of data varies with the size and structure of the sample. At one extreme underwriters will be aware of those risks where the physical characteristics of the risk and the behavioural characteristics of the insured are unique and, to compound the problem, the risk has not been in existence long enough to generate internal loss statistics. Industries which are exploiting new and experimental technologies fall into this category. At the other extreme, there are other risks such as fire insurance on dwellings where the insurers' records are based on very large numbers of clients and stretch back over many years. Between these extremes there lies a plethora of risks for which statistical inference will yield estimates of loss potential of greater or lesser precision.

The cost of utilising information must also be considered. Even if available information permits reliable estimation of future loss probabilities, the factors determining these probabilities may be many and complex. If they are to be fully exploited in premium rating a very expensive administrative system may be required to observe, grade, and record these factors for each insured and then to calculate a suitable premium. Insurance premium structures are therefore a product of compromises between the cost and quality of basic data and compromises between the administrative costs and the competitive benefits of using this data. Whilst these compromises are inevitable, they do not pre-empt criticism where insurers fail to realise the economic value of statistical information or where inefficient rating structures become fossilised through apathy and lack of competitive stimulus.

This chapter considers the case that insurance premiums disseminate information on loss probabilities and on the cost effectiveness of different loss prevention devices.

## Information and optimal expenditure on loss prevention

The capacity of individuals to calculate the probability of suffering loss by fire, theft or the like, and how these probabilities change with different forms of loss prevention, may be expected to vary widely. At one extreme, large firms with multiple exposures and whose experience is monitored by a risk manager may have a fairly good idea of their loss probability distribution. The private houseowner or motorist, however, will have very little idea of the possibility of his house burning down or of his chances of involvement in a motor accident. These uncertainties suggest that, without insurance protection, individuals may not seek their optimal levels of loss prevention.

The effects of imperfect information are illustrated here by Fig. 4.1. Curves $SS$ and $PP$ compare with the cost and demand curves shown in Fig. 2.2 (see p.13) and represent the marginal cost of additional safety devices and the reduction in the expected value of losses respectively. The individual will minimise the combined expected cost of losses and prevention by installing $OZ$ safety devices. However, the effect of uncertainty as to how loss prevention will reduce loss probabilities implies that the individual is unable to specify the curve $PP$. The subjective probability estimates may be represented by a band instead of a single line: this is shown

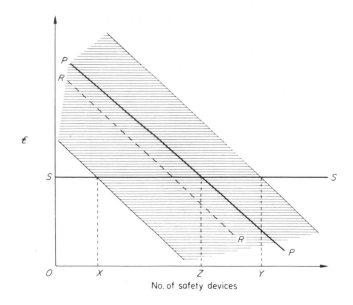

Fig. 4.1    Expenditure on loss prevention under uncertainty

as the shaded area in Fig. 4.1. The width of the band will reflect the degree of uncertainty: those with a high degree of confidence in their subjective estimates will have a narrow band and those with little confidence will have a broad band. Just as important is the positioning of the band. Accurate estimates will tend to centre on PP but other estimates may be so far out that PP may not even lie within the band. With these subjective estimates, the chosen level of loss prevention will lie within the range OX to OY and only by sheer coincidence will it fall at OZ.

The dissemination function works in two ways. First, the individual who is insured need not estimate probabilities: his payback to loss prevention is a premium reduction which may be represented by a single line such as RR. Secondly, it is suggested that the intersection of RR and SS is *more likely* to give a solution closer to OZ than the intuitive and somewhat random selection of a point within the range ȮX and OY. If this is the case, then insurance premiums may be said to convey more accurate information on loss probabilities and changes in these probabilities than is likely to prevail in the absence of insurance.

The plausibility of this hypothesis stems from the insurers' greater access to statistical material. Estimates of the loss probabilities for a risk can be made by reference to (a) historical losses for the risk being considered; (b) subjective judgements; or (c) external data on losses suffered by risks which are similar to the one being considered. Whilst internal historical data may be available to both the insurer and the insured, it is usually of limited value in estimating future loss probabilities. The reason is that, for all but very large risks, there is usually too short a period of exposure or too few units of exposure to generate representative loss experience. Subjective judgements may be inevitable where there is no statistical data but they are usually unreliable because they depend on personal attitudes. Thus the main source of objective data upon which loss probabilities can be estimated is external data from comparable risks.

Access to classified loss data is almost entirely monopolised by insurers who collect and analyse this information in order to devise and monitor their premium rates. Whereas life insurers have traditionally published mortality tables based on their claims experience, non-life insurers have guarded their loss statistics closely. On the other side of the market brokers and insureds have failed to react by providing their own loss statistics. Thus whilst the largest brokers have portfolios of sufficient size to enable them to compile loss statistics comparable with those of many insurance companies, they have nevertheless failed to do so. Nor has this deficiency been made good by insureds. Whilst there has been much discussion of loss data banks on an industry basis, few instances of these pooling arrangements are ever encountered.

On the basis of access to information there appears to be a strong case in support of the hypothesis that insurance premiums disseminate information on loss probabilities. However, it is also important to examine the quality of data and the way in which it is used in insurers' rating structures.

## Insurers' rating systems

Certain factors may be thought to, or known to, affect the expected value of claims for a given insured and also the dispersion of his loss distribution. Some of these factors are easily observable, others are not. In practice, the patent factors are often physical features of the risk and the latent factors are often behavioural features, though some overlaps do arise. For example, consider the fire risk to a factory: it may be affected by the location, the industrial processes which are undertaken there, the type of construction, and the presence of fire detection and extinguishing devices. Relationships between staff and management or the system of work may also be important, but these are difficult to observe or measure. The distinction between these patent and latent factors must rest, in practice, on the training, perception and conventions adopted by the insurance surveyor. The distinction also separates two approaches to insurance rating.

For present purposes, it is useful to divide insurers' rating systems between those which operate on the basis of factors which can be observed and recorded, usually at the time the underwriter decides whether to accept the risk,[1] and those which account for latent factors but infer their potency from the previous experience of the individual risk under a period of insurance protection. In the first case, statistical material may be drawn from sources external to the risk, such as other firms operating in the same industry, but in the second case statistical material is internal and historical. These broad categories are labelled *feature* rating and *experience* rating.[2]

*Feature rating*

Under class rating systems the incentives for loss prevention depend on how broadly the class groupings of insureds are drawn. At one extreme, the rating system might cover very wide categories of insureds who are thought to share similar risk characteristics and who are consequently charged the same rate of premium. A familiar example is household insurance where all dwellings which are constructed of standard materials are charged the same rate of premium.

The implication of using broad risk classes is that they embrace a heterogeneous selection of insureds. Other things being equal, the broader the risk class, the more diverse the risks which are included. The ultimate stage is one in which the rating system contains no room for adjustment to individual risk characteristics so that, no matter what risk improvement is undertaken, the premium will remain unchanged. Something approaching this state is reached in household insurance. The absence of premium incentives thus indicates a social loss with inadequate investment in loss prevention. It also implies a sacrifice of underwriting profit as indicated by the profit model of chapter 3. However, for the insurer this will be offset by a clear saving in the costs of administering such a simple rating structure.

A more complex form of class rating divides a portfolio on the basis of not one, but a number of variables: each permutation of variables forming a separate class. For example, if the relevant features in a property rating scheme were: industry (of which there were one hundred classifications); construction (of which there were five classifications); and sprinkler protection (of which there were four classifications), then there would be $100 \times 5 \times 4 = 2,000$ classes. The ability of such a structure to efficiently discriminate between risks depends upon the size of the portfolio, its distribution over the relevant variables, which variables are selected and the techniques of statistical inference used. The greater the number of variables chosen, the nearer the scheme can potentially approach an appropriate rate for each individual risk. On the other hand, increasing the number of variables causes a combinatorial explosion in the number of cells which have to be treated separately for rating purposes, and correspondingly reduces the number of observations for each cell.

The division of a portfolio into a large number of separate classes introduces the prospect that insureds may move between different classes by use of safety devices, behavioural changes and other forms of loss prevention. However, the discriminatory power of the system, and hence the value of incentives for loss prevention, depends on the accuracy with which the pure premium for each class can be established. Since the loss experience within each narrowly defined cell will be based on a small sample[3] it will provide an unreliable guide to future loss expectancy and rates established on this basis will contain corresponding distortions. An alternative approach is to use multivariate techniques which can examine the influence of individual factors across the whole portfolio and use this collective experience to infer the loss expectancy within each cell. Whilst the problem of interdependence between explanatory variables may cause some difficulty with this approach, there are techniques for monitoring interdependence and multivariate techniques are being increasingly used for improving class rating systems.

The alternative method of adjusting premiums to the observable features of each risk (schedule rating) runs into different problems. Here the important feature is the adoption of a primary classification of risks in order to focus attention on 'standard risk'. The standard risks need not be typical of a wider group but may simply represent a convenient yardstick against which actual risks may be compared. Thus in the Universal Mercantile System in use for fire underwriting in the United States the focus is on a standard building (a high grade one) in a standard town.[4] The alternative Analytic System or Dean Schedule, also in use in the United States, distinguishes between three different types of construction but separates further according to the grading of community protection in the town where the risk is situate.[5] The Fire Offices Committee tariff in the UK identifies standard risks on an industry basis.

But schedule rating systems can and do incorporate substantial premium incentives for certain forms of loss prevention. After identifying the focus risk or standard risk the second stage in rating is to define the individual risk in terms of a schedule of relevant deviations from the standard risk and award a series of premium debits or credits to arrive at a rate for that risk. The adjustments in a typical fire schedule relate to features such as occupancy, hazardous processes, number of stories, construction and type of protection, etc.

The present argument against scheduled rating systems is that they become rigid and insensitive to changing technology – 'the rates are only loosely related to statistical data and the weights assigned to the factors in the schedule are arbitrary'.[6] All three systems mentioned above have been in operation in fundamentally the same form for many decades and the relationships between factors identified in the schedules have remained substantially the same in spite of changing loss experience. 'The general rate level and the rates for broad classes respond to experience, but, and this is particularly true of schedule rates, the rate charged for insurance on a particular risk is not arrived at by statistical process.'[7] Thus, for example, under the FOC tariff the broad adjustment to experience is provided by applying a percentage adjustment for each industry in the light of the industry loss experience. The factors in the schedules remain substantially unchanged. Indeed, the FOC, until recently, had collected no statistics relating to the factors receiving credits and debits in the industry schedules (with the sole exception of sprinklers) and therefore could provide no basis for weighting these factors other than subjective and arbitrary judgement.[8]

Whether or not a feature rating system reflects a serious attempt to relate premium rates to the degree of risk depends largely upon whether the factors identified in the rating structure, and their respective weightings, are based upon, and monitored against, empirical data. There is nothing inherent in a feature rating system which precludes the intensive use of statistical material but the simpler solution, and the one that has invariably been chosen, is to ask whether performance over a broad class of risks is satisfactory. If it is not, then a simple, proportionate, across the board adjustment is made.

*Experience rating*

Experience rating does attempt to relate premiums payable by each insured to the loss expectancy for that insured (this being estimated from his past loss record). This method is commonly used for private motor insurance, where the number and timing of the insured's recent claims will determine his placing on a no claims discount (NCD) scale, and in motor fleet and employers' liability insurances where a common method of rating for large risks is to charge a premium based upon the previous three to five years' losses adjusted for trend and with a mark-up for reserve contributions, overheads and profit. Furthermore, since there is an implied threat that insurers will be prepared to increase any premium (or withdraw cover) if claims experience becomes exceptionally poor, then experience

51

rating exists in a latent form in all rating systems.

The advantage of this system is that, since there is a relationship, albeit random, between current activity to reduce losses and future loss experience, the system contains inbuilt incentives for loss prevention. These inducements require no prescience on the part of the insurer – he need make no selection as to which factors are relevant nor any judgement as to how relevant they are. The system is automatic and flexible. Yet another aspect of the flexibility of experience rating is that it can be superimposed on another rating structure, e.g. class or schedule rating, and thereby provide inducement for types of loss prevention which are not anticipated in the main rating system. Probably the main advantage of experience rating is that it takes account of behavioural characteristics of the insured which may not be observable and cannot be included in a feature rating system and yet are highly relevant in determining the probability and severity of loss.

In all cases of estimation of loss probabilities from claims data, reliability depends on the size and quality of the sample from which the data is drawn. Thus, on the one hand, the larger the sample, the smaller the distortions due to the random timing and distribution of losses. On the other hand, care must be taken to see that data is relevant to the risk in question; thus the driver's claims record of thirty years ago is unlikely to be of much help in calculating current loss expectancies. In private motor insurance the typical compromise between relevance and minimising random disturbance is to take into account claims experience for the previous five or six years. Since, in statistical terms, this is a small sample it becomes very difficult to separate the degree to which the accident record is due to inherently risky features or to pure chance. This is illustrated by the following simplified example. Suppose that a no claims discount increases each year for five years, but if a claim is made all discount is lost. Further, there are two types of driver: safe drivers who have a five in six chance of surviving each year without a claim, and inherently bad drivers who have a two in three chance of surviving each year without a claim. If the same people are insured in the portfolio year after year (no new policyholders and no one dropping out) then the portfolio will settle down to a pattern in which about one-quarter of those on maximum discount will be bad drivers and about one-third of those on no discount will be good drivers.[9]

The use of experience rating in private motor insurance may provide a relatively inefficient tool for relating premiums to expected claims values and for monitoring changes in loss expectancy. However, it is significant that it is used in conjunction with a feature rating scheme which distinguishes between factors such as make of car, age of driver, occupation and location. The particular value of the no claims discount scheme is that it picks up the behavioural factors ignored by feature rating.

With other branches of insurance the use of experience rating may not encounter such serious problems of sample size. In employers' liability the labour force at risk may, in some cases, run into many thousands. Although these employees are not strictly independently exposed to the risk of injury, the loss experience of such a large labour force over a period of, say, two or three years may provide a fairly reliable basis for estimating future loss expectancy. Likewise with a large fleet of motor vehicles.

However, the flexibility of experience rating is not without its costs. Whilst it economises on the detail of knowledge required by the insurer in order to devise premium incentives for loss prevention, it correspondingly conveys little or no hard information to the insured as to what type, and how much, loss prevention to undertake. It was suggested at the beginning of this chapter that insurers might act as a clearing house for factual information on the effectiveness of different loss prevention devices. Whereas feature rating systems have a role to play in disseminating information on the cost effectiveness of specific devices, experience rating systems merely convey a vague and generalised inducement to care. Furthermore, the loss prevention incentives under feature rating are in the form of a certainty payback for undertaking a specific course of action. With experience rating the payback is highly speculative: i.e. a possible reduction in the number or severity of losses over those which would have prevailed in the absence of loss prevention and the consequent implications for premiums. A third problem arises through the timing of costs and benefits. Since the productivity of loss prevention is only measured through subsequent experience, there will be a lag before measurement can take place and this may be very considerable. The insured may be less likely to invest in loss prevention where the return is both future and uncertain than he would if the return were in the form of an immediate premium reduction. The potency of the incentives under an experience rating scheme depends on the insured's trade off between present and future income.

## Subjective rating

Subjective rating may be considered as a system in its own right or it may refer to the personal judgements which creep into any rating system. There are risks which are rated without any recourse to statistical material either because it is not available or because it is not appropriate. It is usually the new and unusual risks which fall into this category. However, no rating system is devoid of these judgements no matter how firm the empirical base. Under feature rating systems an underwriter has to compare individual risks with those from which loss data is drawn – this comparison inevitably requires subjective judgement. Even the techniques available for inferring future probabilities from past data require judgements to be made and these judgements can have a significant impact on the quality of processed material.

Whilst subjective rating may introduce flexibility into otherwise rigid rating structures, it is also clear that they reflect not only the objective quality of the risk but also the psychological traits of the underwriter. The value of subjective judgement in terms of efficient incentives for loss prevention depends both on personalities and on the background against which they are made. It may be supposed that where they are used to displace rather than to interpret or supplement empirical data the discriminatory power of the rating system will, in general, deteriorate.


## The dissemination of information

Whilst the basic statistics upon which premiums are based are not normally made available to insurance buyers, it is essential for the concept of dissemination that the information contained in premium differentials is available to the insured. Ideally, what is required is that, first, the insured should have access to information for premium adjustments following changes in the risk from his insurer and, secondly, he should also be aware of differences in premiums and adjustments for risk improvement between insurers. At first sight it may seem that even the first of these conditions is not met since insurers' rating manuals are often considered to be confidential internal documents. This constraint may be overcome following an insurance survey since this often contains suggestions for risk improvement. The issue depends upon the extent to which insurers see their surveyors as providing a loss prevention advisory service as opposed to the traditional function of providing rating information to the underwriter. (This is considered further in the next chapter.)

For risks which are handled by brokers both the first and second conditions should be met. It is the function of brokers to have an in-depth knowledge of insurance premium structures and to use this knowledge to compile the best insurance package for their clients. A large section of the insurance market falls into this category. For example, it has been estimated that about 75 per cent of non-life commercial and industrial business and about 90 per cent of marine and pension business is handled by brokers. However, brokers handle about 30 per cent of ordinary life and private motor business and a somewhat lower proportion of household insurance.[10] Whilst the nature of their function suggests that they will convey the appropriate premium information to the insured, brokers do face a conflict of interests. Brokerage is invariably calculated as a percentage of premiums and, consequently, loss prevention will reduce the broker's income. The force of this constraint depends both on the integrity of the broker and the intensity of competition for business. This conflict might be resolved in time by the evolution of alternative methods of renumeration such as the negotiation of a fee related to the quality of advice and the work done, but at the present time these arrangements are the exception rather than the rule.

For their part, insurers appear to be more concerned with technical advice than with giving information on the financial inducements to loss prevention. This has been particularly noticeable in the establishment of agencies such as the Fire Protection Association and the Central Fire Liaison Panel, and in the promotion of research and in the surveying of risks. Whilst insurers may be forgiven some self-congratulation for these various exercises, they will not, with the exception of surveying, be considered in more detail in this study. Insurers only allocate a tiny proportion of their income to these activities, whereas the source of concern here is with the incentives created, and the information generated, by their main activity as insurers.

The hypothesis that insurers act as a sort of clearing house for information on loss probabilities and disseminate information on loss prevention in the form of premium differentials is not of an 'all or nothing' nature. Premium adjustments never perfectly reflect differences in loss probabilities due to imperfections in loss data, problems of statistical inference, the rigidities of rating structures and the failure to give premium data universal circulation. Whilst these problems can never be entirely removed, they can be lessened by careful investigation and planning. The important issues here are whether the information in premium structures provides a more reliable guide to loss expectancies than the subjective estimates of insureds and whether the information which is available, or potentially available, is efficiently exploited. The answer to the first of these issues clearly depends very much on the answer given to the second; this is therefore taken up with reference to particular insurance markets in the following chapters.

**Notes**

[1] An exception is retrospective rating. For example, the size of the employer's payroll gives one indication of the magnitude of the risk for employers' liability insurance but it cannot be measured accurately until the period of insurance has expired. Consequently, an estimate may be made at inception and an adjustment following the closure of the period of insurance.

[2] This classification is adopted for convenience. An alternative classification commonly used is between class rating (some convenient criterion is used to divide the portfolio into subgroups and, though each subgroup has a different rate, each risk within a subgroup has the same rate) and individual rating (where risks are not standardised into rating groups but are treated separately for rating purposes). See, for example, H.S. Denenberg et al., *Risk and Insurance,* Prentice Hall, Englewood Cliffs 1964, chs. 26 and 27.

[3] A similar example is given by P.J. Hall, 'The motor risks statistics bureau', *Journal of the Chartered Insurance Institute,* vol.70, 1973.

[4] See R.I. Mehr and E. Cammack, *Principles of Insurance,* 5th ed., R.D. Irwin, Homewood 1972, pp.653–4, and D.L. Bicklehaupt, *General Insurance,* 9th ed., R.D. Irwin, Homewood 1974, pp.150–1.

[5] Mehr and Cammack, op.cit., p.654–5 and Bicklehaupt, op.cit., p.151.

[6] See T.C. Allen and R.M. Duval, *Property Insurance Rating – A Plea for Change,* American Society of Insurance Management, New York 1973, chapter 3.

[7] A.H. Mowbray and R.H. Blanchard, *Insurance – Its Theory and Practice in the United States,* 5th ed., McGraw-Hill, 1961, p.389.

[8] See chapter 5.

[9] For another example with a more complex bonus scheme, see P.D. Johnson and G.B. Hey, 'Statistical studies in motor insurance', *Journal of the Institute of Actuaries,* vol.97, part 2, no.407, December 1971. See also chapter 6.

[10] *Insurance: Profile of An Industry,* Corporation of Insurance Brokers, London 1968.

# 5 Fire insurance pricing and loss prevention

In 1973 direct fire losses in the United Kingdom accounted for a little over 0·3 per cent of the Gross National Product[1] and, though there are difficulties in making international comparisons, the percentage for the United States was roughly of the same order.[2] This figure relates to the estimated material damage by fire and, if other costs attributable to fire or its prevention such as the costs of protection, fire brigades, administering insurance, loss of life etc. are added, then the cost of fire reaches about 1·1 per cent of GNP.[3] Further addition should be made for indirect losses such as lost production. Estimates vary widely as to how significant this consequential loss may be. Intuitive estimates given by risk managers range from ratios of 2:1 (consequential loss to direct loss) to 4:1. If these losses were simply added together a certain amount of double counting would occur since some of the lost production of one firm due to a fire would be taken up by rival firms with spare capacity. The ratio of 1½:1 probably gives a conservative estimate of consequential loss due to fire and if this is added to the other costs of fire the total expressed as a percentage of GNP is something over 1½ per cent. In absolute values the figure is about £950 million.

Relating fire loss to GNP reveals how much of the wealth being created each year is diverted to financing fire losses: the figure expressed in the preceding paragraph is certainly alarmingly high. Furthermore, for the UK, the proportion of GNP allocated to fire costs has been increasing, as is shown in Fig. 5.1. This trend stands in contrast to experience in the United States and Canada where the trend appears to be declining: experience in Western Europe is somewhat varied and comparisons between major nations are difficult due to the relative paucity of data.

Perhaps a more useful way of examining trends in fire losses is to relate wastage to the value of assets of risk. If the degree of hazard measured in this way were constant, then an increasing trend in the ratio of fire wastage/GNP could be explained simply by capital stock growing faster than national income. However, even using this measure, the trend in fire hazard, although subject to wide fluctuations, appears to be of an upwards direction as can be seen from Fig. 5.2.

Fire and fire prevention consume a conspicuously large proportion of

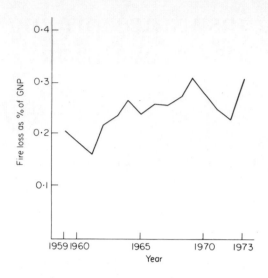

Fig. 5.1　Direct fire loss as a percentage of GNP for the United Kingdom

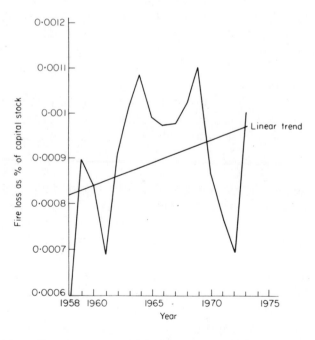

Fig. 5.2　Direct fire loss as a percentage of national capital stock (at current replacement cost) for the United Kingdom

58

our national resources and the problem is growing. The economics of fire prevention is properly concerned with the reduction of the *total* cost of fire by exploiting interdependencies between prevention costs and fire wastage. This chapter examines the role played by fire insurers in this economic process.

## The United Kingdom fire insurance market

The analysis of the preceding chapters leaves us with a range of competing hypotheses. At one extreme, the process of risk transfer destroys incentives for loss prevention and there are no compensating incentives in the premium structure. On the other hand, insurance may play a passive role by replacing incentives removed by risk transfer by offsetting incentives in the premium structure. Cutting across these is another set of hypotheses focussing not on incentives but on information. Insurance rating may be empirically based so that premiums convey accurate information on loss prevention or, alternatively, it may be arbitrary, in which case information on loss prevention may be non-existent or misleading. In order to choose between these hypotheses it is necessary to examine the market structure and its effects on both premium discrimination and the provision of information.

One of the important indicators of the degree of competition prevailing in different industries is the proportion of industry output accounted for by the largest firms. Using these measures, known as the concentration ratios, it is estimated that in 1972 the largest firm in the United Kingdom fire insurance market accounted for some 13 per cent of market output; the top five firms accounted for 47 per cent of output; and the top ten firms accounted for around 64 per cent of industry output.[4] However, even this measure understates the degree of centralisation in pricing decisions since many of the companies support a collective pricing agreement.

In discussing market structures in the United States, C. Arthur Williams has distinguished three common types: those with a single bureau membership of which is compulsory and deviations from whose rates are not permitted; those where bureau membership is compulsory but deviations are permitted; and those where membership is optional and deviations are permitted.[5] In view of the central role played by the Fire Offices Committee (FOC) the United Kingdom fire insurance market is seen to resemble the third category. The FOC members account for approximately 62 per cent of UK direct fire premium income. Membership of the FOC is heavily weighted in favour of the larger companies. Unfortunately, published statistics are somewhat out of date but in 1970 the thirty-eight tariff companies operating included the top three companies and accounted for about 63 per cent of the market output. Sixty-seven non-tariff companies accounted for about 30 per cent of the market premium income and the residual was accounted for by Lloyd's.

The tariff is fairly typical of restrictive price agreements encountered in other industries. It is an agreement between members to enforce a set of minimum rates which are based upon statistics pooled by members. Deviations from tariff rates are not normally permitted by members but independent insurers are free to charge what they wish. Competition from non-tariff insurers provides a potential constraint on the freedom of the tariff bloc to control prices and conditions of insurance. From this market framework has emerged a complex market structure and an equally complex structure of premium rating.

However, whilst it is normally assumed that restrictive price agreements are formed to reap monopoly profits, the FOC has recently revealed the principles upon which it fixes rates in defending its case to the Monopolies Commission. The FOC declared that '. . . the equitable distribution of cost is one of the fundamental principles governing the operation of the tariff system'.[6] This objective is based upon (a) the public interest and (b) the FOC's constitutional commitment 'To promote sound practice in the transaction of insurance . . .'.[7] The term 'sound practice' could well summarise the analysis described in chapter 3 which revealed a distinct profit advantage for insurers, collectively as well as individually, to devise a pricing structure which discriminates between insureds according to the marginal costs each imposes on the insurance fund. However, in spite of this commitment, it cannot automatically be concluded that the FOC pricing structure transmits an efficient set of incentives for loss prevention. Distortions may occur, first, where the pricing structure fails to achieve an appropriate allocation of claims costs between different insureds and, secondly, where the allocation of insurers' expenses and other costs also fails to distinguish efficiently the costs imposed on the fund by each insured.

### The allocation of claims costs between insureds

Since the main basis for rating has been the claims premium ratio (with little further subdivision than industrial class and whether protected by sprinklers) the FOC has severely handicapped itself in the collection of statistical material. The supporting material consisted of details of large fires and further information from the member making the largest loss returns for each class but this information has apparently not been scientifically used. Consequently, the scheduled credits and debits for individual features of the risk are mainly subjective judgements with very little statistical backing; the penalties or discounts appear to have been arbitrary responses where certain features have played a conspicuous part in causing or aggravating certain large fires or where laboratory experiments have displayed that particular features respond in particular ways. Thus, until recently, the FOC had not undertaken any systematic collection of data for the majority of factors relevant to premium rating.

The arbitrary nature of premium adjustments can be seen clearly through the procedures for revising rates.[8] The FOC sets target loss ratios on an industry basis. If claims experience for any particular industry changes, the tariff basic rate and adjustments in the schedule remain intact but are subject to an overall percentage mark-up (known as a SOPA – Schedule of Percentage Adjustment) which is varied to achieve the target loss ratio.

The operation of this system with respect to sprinkler installations is curious. The normal pattern is to give a constant minus 20 per cent adjustment or, in a few cases, to exempt the sprinklered property from SOPA altogether. This means that rates for sprinklered properties are largely invariant with respect to changing claims experience for the industry (sprinklered and unsprinklered properties) as a whole and also that the effective adjustment for installing sprinklers varies very widely and erratically as the industry claims experience changes.[9]

There is a chance that many of these problems may soon disappear for, as the Monopolies Commission was conducting its enquiry, the FOC was setting up a much more intensive system for collecting loss information.[10] From 1970 onwards, offices have been returning statistical information on other factors which are rateable, e.g. construction, height, undivided floor area, combustible ceilings and linings, and protection (including not only sprinklers but also ordinary appliances and fire alarm systems). This sort of information could lead to more efficient discrimination in the rating structure, and it remains to be seen how the FOC will use this information.

## The allocation of expenses between insureds

The monopoly power implied by a tariff structure may be used to raise the general level of prices. The high price level might produce large profit margins or, alternatively, it may promote inefficiency by protecting high cost producers.[11] It is clearly evident from published data that profits of FOC members in recent years have not been high relative to other industries and the Monopolies Commission itself endorses this view.[12] However, the price level docs support a large differential between aggregate claims and premiums. In terms of the analysis of chapter 2, the form of the premium loading is just as important as its absolute size, and, since the FOC uses target loss ratios to set its premium levels, the loading appears to be a proportionate one.[13]

Selected claims/premiums ratios for the period 1963–73 are shown in Table 5.1. The reason for the fluctuations appears to be random fluctuations in the incidence of claims and, in recent years, the difficulties in forecasting claims costs during a period of accelerating inflation, coupled with unexpected increases in the number of claims. However, after having adjusted to the new trends in fire losses, the FOC has now set its premium levels in accordance with a target loss ratio of 50 per cent, and this, in the view of the Monopolies Commission, will lead to excessively high rates of profit.[14]

Apart from the effect on profits, the tariff structure is also likely to support a set of costs and commissions at higher levels than would prevail under a competitive structure. The tariff rates of premium would have to be pitched at such a level as to be acceptable to the least efficient member. Whilst the Commission could find no evidence to suggest that the efficiency of manpower usage in the insurance industry was less than that of other major employers of clerical labour, it is significant to note that the independent companies were able to operate at lower expense/premium ratios, even though their premiums were generally lower than those of the tariff companies.

Premium loadings are of the general order of 40–50 per cent of premiums paid. If these loadings were assumed to be fairly constant as between different classes of property, usage and protection, then insurance would have systematic effects on the level of expenditure on loss prevention. First, the expected level of expenditure under insurance protection would probably be higher than under self-insurance. With loadings pitched at 50 per cent of the actuarial value at risk, the premium reduction is double the reduction in the expected value of claims. Furthermore, if it is also assumed that the efficient allocation of overheads is achieved by a combination loading, as suggested in chapter 2, then a proportionate loading structure may be expected to lead to socially excessive expenditures on loss prevention. However, these conclusions depend upon an

Table 5.1

Summary of claims incurred as percentages of premiums earned, 1963–73

| | 1963 | 1964 | 1965 | 1966 | 1967 | 1968 | 1969 | 1970 | 1971 | 1972 | 1973 |
|---|---|---|---|---|---|---|---|---|---|---|---|
| Domestic: | | | | | | | | | | | |
| Tariff offices | 89·2 | 30·8 | 34·9 | 33·4 | 28·7 | 43·8 | 32·1 | 29·8 | – | – | – |
| Independent offices | 76·2 | 33·4 | 31·0 | 34·6 | 27·2 | 46·5 | 35·1 | – | – | – | – |
| Non-domestic: | | | | | | | | | | | |
| Tariff offices | 77·5 | 67·8 | 63·6 | 58·6 | 55·4 | 68·9 | 63·2 | 41·9 | – | – | – |
| Independent offices | 76·2 | 62·0 | 65·2 | 61·1 | 64·5 | 74·5 | 71·7 | – | – | – | – |
| Total: | | | | | | | | | | | |
| Tariff offices | 81·5 | 55·1 | 53·8 | 50·1 | 46·3 | 60·7 | 53·9 | 38·6 | – | 44·9 | 56·7 |
| Independent offices | 77·7 | 51·5 | 54·3 | 51·8 | 52·6 | 63·0 | 59·8 | – | – | 55·8 | 51·0 |

Source: 1963–70 – Monopolies Commission, twenty selected companies.
1972–73 – Analysis of Department of Trade returns of the top ten companies.

accurate distribution of claims costs between different insureds. The use of rules of thumb and subjective judgements in calculating premiums implies that the risk premium charged to each insured will be somewhat erratic and, consequently, the use of a proportionate mark-up may only serve to enhance these random disturbances.

### Competition – the role of non-tariff insurers

Whilst the FOC restrains price competition amongst its members, there is also a large non-tariff sector comprising Lloyds', which accounts for about 7 per cent of total market premiums, and independent companies, accounting for a further 30 per cent of market premium income. These insurers are not bound by FOC regulations; they are in the advantageous position of being able to attract business away from the tariff bloc by undercutting tariff rates and they have undoubtedly exploited this position. Apart from reducing the general level of rates, the independent companies might have been able to attract business with low loss expectancy away from the tariff by grouping insureds into small and more homogeneous units and thereby stimulating the FOC to revise its own rating system. However, whilst some competition of this nature undoubtedly does occur, particularly on the part of Lloyds', it is not on a sufficient scale to threaten the tariff or to force the FOC to revise its rating structure.

The rating structures operated by the majority of non-tariff insurers are parasitic. Most of the independent companies freely admitted to the Monopolies Commission that they set their own rates after taking account '. . . not only of the rate which would be charged by the tariff companies, but also of the detailed components of the rate and of the FOC standards on which they are based'.[15] There are three reasons for this strategy. First, most independent insurers have portfolios which are too small to produce reliable statistics. As mentioned above, the tariff companies are typically larger than the independents. Secondly, the collection, analysis and implementation of statistical information is a costly process and the independent insurers have been able to avoid these costs by basing their own rates around the tariff. Thirdly, many fire insurance risks are beyond the underwriting capacity of individual insurers and it is therefore common practice for insurers to underwrite risks collectively, each taking that percentage (line) which they feel is acceptable. This form of co-operation is facilitated by standard policy conditions and similar rating methods. The usual procedure is for non-tariff insurers simply to discount the tariff rate by a certain percentage.

A further restraint on the expansion of non-tariff insurers is the 63/35 rule enforced by the tariff.[16] Under this rule, tariff insurers may not participate in a collective policy in which more than 35 per cent is allocated to non-tariff insurers. The potency of this rule lies both in the need for co-operation between insurers and the fact that very many fire risks are considered to be beyond the underwriting capacity of the independent companies as a group. Consequently, the rule is rigidly enforced.

The constraints on competition are also vividly illustrated by American experience. The structure of fire insurance rating in the United Kingdom has many parallels with practice in the United States. The normal basis for rating is a scheduled rating system and two forms in particular are in widespread use: the Dean, or Analytic, Schedule, and the Universal Mercantile System.[17] Each of these systems established a basis rate for a standard risk and contained a schedule of debits and credits for deviations from the standard. The main difference between the two systems is that under the Dean Schedule the adjustments are proportional to the basis rate, whereas under the Universal Mercantile System they are flat rate additions or subtractions to the basis rate. In the case of sprinklers in particular, there are substantial discounts which may be as large as 80 per cent of the unsprinklered rate.

The problems are illustrated by a consideration of the Dean Schedule. Dean himself suggested that the relative contributions of the various factors were constant and that the effect of including this assumption in the schedule was to concentrate underwriters' attention on the adequacies of the final rate produced by the system. In its application, too, the relativities between the various factors have also tended to be frozen. Insurers have maintained control over their underwriting performance merely by setting a target ratio of expected claims to premiums and choosing a multiple of the basic rate for the class to achieve this.[18]

Not only is the analytic schedule inflexible but the set of relativities between the different base rates and schedule adjustments is also founded on arbitrary judgements concerning the contributions of the various factors. This is accepted by one writer who, in spite of his more general thesis that the system produces rates which are fairly discriminatory, concedes that 'On the other hand, the specific credits and debits in the schedule must be based upon judgment and are not testable, and intangible factors cannot be handled satisfactorily.'[19] The assumption that the contribution is not capable of empirical validation and that testing must certainly be in doubt has been vigorously challenged recently by T.C. Allen and R.M. Duval.[20] Their recent and detailed case study of one particular industry focusses on particular factors in the rating structure and compares premiums with claims frequencies. Their analysis casts doubt not only on the relativities between the rating factors but also on the whole structure.

The survival in America of an inflexible and arbitrary system such as the Dean Schedule and the Universal Mercantile System is undoubtedly due, as in Britain, to the cartel structure in the supply of insurance. Although an increasing volume of business is being transacted independently of the rating bureaus,[21] they have historically been a dominant feature in fire insurance markets. Furthermore, whilst the conduct of fire insurance business is subject to state regulation, in some cases state control has fostered the bureau system. In some states membership of a rating bureau is obligatory, whereas in others deviation from bureau rates requires specific approval. In terms of the analysis of chapter 3, this structure denies the competitive pressures to establish an empirical foundation for existing rating factors and to search for new ones. The structure is not conducive to innovation in loss prevention. Whilst these benefits may be expected to flow from a more competitive structure, it is as well to first look more closely at the objectives of state regulation.

The bargaining position of rating bureaus *vis-à-vis* state legislatures has undoubtedly been enhanced by widespread fears that unbridled competition would lead to price wars and insolvencies. The need to protect the public from insolvencies has consequently been a competing objective with the need to protect insureds from monopolistic practices, in particular the reaping of excess profits. Furthermore, unlike British regulation of the solvency of insurance companies (which focuses directly on the adequacy of reserves), US state regulation operates directly on the level and structure of rates. Rates should neither be so low as to imperil solvency nor so high as to yield excessive profits. These factors have led not only to a tolerance of rating bureaus but in some states an active encouragement of them.

State legislation, based on the All Industry Bills approved by the National Association of Insurance Commissioners in 1946, is generally required to ensure that rates are 'not unfairly discriminatory'. This is generally interpreted to mean that the rates applying to individual insureds should, as far as possible, be proportional to the expected claims cost.[22] Although this is not the optimal structure in terms of incentives for loss prevention, it may nevertheless be considered to imply a fairly efficient system. The policing of such a system by the insurance commissioners is another matter and it is doubtful whether many state commissioners departments have sufficient administrative capacity or technical skills to supervise such a system.[23]

The correct inference from this discussion is not that competition does not exist in the United States but rather that in most areas it has been insufficient to break down the rigid and uniform rating systems.[24] However, one of the interesting features of the market is the size and success of specialist insurers who concentrate on 'highly protected risks'. The two large associations which operate in this market are the Factory Mutual System and the Factory Insurers Association, both of which practise a highly selective underwriting procedure concentrating on high standard risks. Consequently, their rates are normally permitted to deviate from the standards adopted by the state regulatory departments. Furthermore, their underwriting activities are backed up by intensive inspecting services and testing and research facilities. These deviating insurers offer an alternative to the more conventional underwriters. Whilst their operations, if viewed in isolation, may appear equally rigid to those of the conventional market, they nevertheless introduce an element of consumer choice and may lead to a more efficient system of incentives for loss prevention.

With price competition apparently increasing, there are signs that the rigid bureau rating systems may give way to more discriminatory systems which more accurately reflect the cost effectiveness of different forms of loss prevention. Significantly, several states have recently enacted 'open competition' rating laws which rely more heavily on competition than state intervention to produce 'proper' premium rates. The common features of these rating laws are: (a) that they recognise the advantages of pooling statistics to produce a more credible base for rating and therefore permit rating bureaus to produce advisory rates; but (b) that agreement between insurers to adhere to these rates is outlawed. Tentative studies of experience under at least two of these laws suggest that insurer conduct shows some reflection of the pressures described in the competitive pricing model in chapter 3.[25] However, the experience is much too recent to provide anything like a full appraisal of these new approaches.

**An alternative market structure**

In discussing premium loadings and premium discrimination, it has been implicitly assumed that the alternative to bureau rating is a competitive market structure and the analysis of this paper has further suggested that this would lead to finer groupings of insureds in a more efficient discriminatory rating structure. Whilst the prediction of what might prevail is a difficult and hazardous affair, it is nonetheless necessary to consider here whether this sort of competitive pressure would ensue. In Britain the independent companies have failed to provide this sort of competition under the present tariff structure – why should it occur without the tariff?

In defending the tariff to the Monopolies Commission, the FOC predicted that if it were dissolved, then insurers 'will not only give varying allowances [for improvements in the risk], but will be driven by competition into giving the allowances in cases where standards are incompletely observed. This, it is said, is likely to become a cumulative process with the result that both incentive and observance will be eroded'.[26] However, the Commission's view is entirely consistent with the analysis of chapters 2 and 3: 'And since all insurers would not be offering identical terms, there would be a greater inducement than under the tariff system for insureds to seek alternative quotations and, in the process, to become more alive to the advantages of adopting fire prevention measures'.[27] Both of these predictions suggest an increase in price competition but, whereas the first suggests that insurers will accommodate business at unprofitable rates of premium, the second suggests that insurers will more accurately divide their portfolio into appropriate risk groups and achieve a more efficient allocation of claims costs between these groups.

Whilst the dissolution of the cartel may be expected to lead to increased price competition, there are other constraints which should preclude the destructive competition forecast by the FOC but which may also limit the pressures for discriminatory rating. First, the need for co-operation between insurers on collective schedules will continue; the system relies on the confidence of the following insurers in the underwriting terms of the leading office. This is likely to bring some standardisation of both rates and policy conditions and, in addition, it will spread information about the rating structures of rivals. Secondly, insurers whose underwriting practices become unsound are unlikely to be able to renegotiate reinsurance treaties and will find their underwriting capacity diminishing. Thirdly, government regulation of solvency requirements has become more onerous over recent years and its watchfulness has been heightened by recent collapses such as those of the Vehicle and General and the Nation Life. These restraints are likely to lead to differential degrees of competition according to the size of risk with, at one end, a form of tacit collusion in the market for large risks but much more freedom of action for individual insurers in the market for small and medium size risks.

The incentives to innovate with new rating structures and differing premium adjustments for loss prevention devices in a 'post-tariff' market would be complex. The abolition of a common standard for all rating would force insurers into a closer examination of their cost structures and a serious consideration of alternative pricing methods. On the other side of the market, the abolition of a common standard would lead brokers and buyers to seek out differences in the rates and conditions of different insurers. These pressures certainly point to a rationalisation of premium incentives. Furthermore, the first two factors mentioned in the preceding paragraph sufficiently differentiate the fire market from the motor market, in which the collapse of tariff was followed by a price war, to suggest that price competition would be less reckless and more solidly based on actuarial considerations. It would be very surprising indeed if insurers had not learnt anything from the motor market experience. However, the same two features of the fire market also lead to ambiguous conclusions concerning the incentive to innovate and the spread of innovation in the market for large risks. If a rating innovation produced by one insurer is considered to be actuarially and commercially unsound, then it may be difficult to allocate a line on collective schedule to that insurer. It will certainly be impossible to allocate the lead to that insurer. However, if the innovation was considered actuarially sound by other insurers, then it is likely to be adopted by competing insurers. The incentives to innovate are counteracted by the need for caution, particularly in selecting the lead underwriter, but it is unlikely that such a system would be as rigid as the tariff structure and, certainly for smaller risks, the incentives for rating innovation are likely to be less restrained.

Innovation needs both incentive and information. Whilst the FOC has been criticised for failing to exploit the mass of statistical data potentially available, it nevertheless provides a convenient structure for pooling data. For small companies, the loss of access to a collective pool of statistics would be a very serious blow. Unless they were highly specialised, say, to a particular industry, they would be forced to find new price leaders to replace the tariff. Many of the larger companies do have portfolios of sufficient size to offer an independent statistical base for rate making but even their records provide a much smaller sample than that available in a collective pool. Whilst the abolition of the practice of collective rating may provide the incentive for more discriminatory rating structures, the abolition of a collective pool of statistics implies a loss of information upon which more refined structures can be based. In the UK motor insurance market collective pooling of statistics has continued after the collapse of the tariff and in America the open competition rating laws aim at a similar structure. It is therefore both possible and feasible for United Kingdom fire insurance that the functions of collective rating and collective pooling of statistics could be divorced.[28] In this case, the advantages of a competitive structure need not be offset by a corresponding loss of information.

## The surveying of risks

In all but small risks it is usual for insurers to conduct a fire survey. Even on the narrowest definition of the survey function this provides the required information to the underwriter to rate the risk in terms of the tariff or other rating manual. However, many insurers see the role of the surveyor as something more than this. Many relevant features of an individual risk cannot be anticipated in a formal rating document and the surveyor is required to introduce flexibility into the rating system by seeking out these individual features. Unlike many of the credits and debits in the rating manual, these adjustments are not based on statistical association but rather on technical judgements made by the surveyor. Consequently, their value depends on the surveyor's personal skills. In this context, it is important to note that fire surveyors in the United Kingdom are typically recruited from a non-technical background and receive little formal training.

An even broader interpretation of the surveyor's function is that, in addition to providing internal information to underwriters and statisticians, he also provides a loss prevention advisory service to the insured. Whilst surveyors' reports have traditionally been considered as confidential internal documents, some insurers claim that they are now more open about their contents and are more willing to make recommendations for risk improvement.

The broadening of their role is in evidence in a sample survey of surveyors' report forms. The sample comprised 400 reports from two very large tariff fire offices. The reports were selected randomly from the period 1950–73. Constraints on the size and design of the survey precluded a large scale random sample and consequently the implications drawn are illustrative rather than strong conclusions. The results show that:

(1)  On those risks which are tariff rated, about 40 per cent of the recommendations related to features not specified in the tariff. These required subjective judgements to be made by the surveyor.
(2)  Surveyors are less willing than in the past to accept a risk as it is and merely leave rating to the underwriter. Fig. 5.3 shows a declining proportion of risks passing through the survey stage without recommendations for improvement being made.
(3)  Although this is more difficult to quantify than the previous point, it is discernible that underwriters are now far more willing not only to pass on the surveyor's recommendations to the insured but to reinforce these by

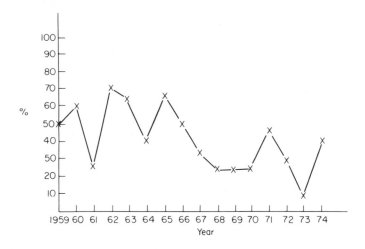

Fig. 5.3    Percentage of surveys in which no recommendations for risk improvement were made

supporting with rate reductions/increases or even declining the insurance. Insurers are less willing to hold back recommendation for fear of souring a relationship with a customer or broker.

Whilst it is important in terms of the information approach outlined in chapter 4 that information in the rating structure is conveyed to the insured, just how much further surveyors can go in offering impartial advice on loss prevention is a matter of some dispute. However, it has been convincingly argued that without a technical background and professional qualifications, surveyors can do little more than advise on so called 'simple' risks.[29] High technology risks call for a more specialised service.

The depth of the advisory service provided by fire insurers in the UK may be further illustrated by contrast with the 'highly protected risk' (HPR) approach commonly found in the United States and the practice in engineering insurance in the United Kingdom. The HPR concept embodies the provision of both insurance and loss prevention services in a single package. The major operators – the Factory Mutual System and the Factory Insurers Association – have teams of highly trained graduate fire and sprinkler engineers who undertake regular and intensive inspections, and, as stated above, the scheme normally limits insurance coverage to very high standard risks. Comparison of the percentage of premium income allocated to surveying/inspection services between FMS insurers

71

and conventional insurers gives some indication of the relative depth of loss prevention services. Under the Factory Mutual System approximately 25 per cent of premium income is allocated to loss prevention services,[30] whereas the comparative figure for conventional UK fire insurers is probably in the region of 1–3 per cent.[31]

Comparing fire with other types of risk is hazardous since the technical problems involved are very different. However, the contrast between the estimated 1–3 per cent of premium income spent by fire insurers on inspection services and the equivalent figure of 30–40 per cent for engineering insurers[32] is so large as to reveal a fundamental difference in emphasis. The contrast between engineering and fire (or other) branches of insurance is revealed in the following plea: 'Perhaps as loss prevention and control as a discipline gain further ground throughout our industry, so also will the demand for surveyors in all areas to have professional qualifications and accountability'.[33]

## Sprinklers – an illustration of incentives for fire protection

One of the most effective ways of reducing fire losses in buildings is sprinkler protection. In a survey of fires in one particular industry in the United States, Allen and Duval show that 'The sprinkler fire rate is approximately 1/6th of the rate for unsprinklered units'.[34] The Fire Protection Association in the UK claims that: 'In general, of all fires occurring in protected premises, about ninety-six per cent are extinguished or controlled by the sprinkler systems. Of the remaining four per cent, many have occurred at a time when the sprinkler system was temporarily closed down for repairs'.[35] Fire brigade statistics confirm the effectiveness of sprinklers, though at a more modest level than that claimed by the FPA. Thus of 1,888 fires in sprinklered premises in the UK in 1971 just over half were small fires which were promptly extinguished. Of the remainder, 79 per cent were controlled or extinguished by the sprinklers.[36]

The effectiveness of sprinkler installations is recognised in most premium structures by the award of substantial premium discounts. Thus under FOC rules the premium discount for a high standard sprinkler installation is normally in the region of 40–60 per cent of the premium. However, since sprinklered premises usually receive a −20 per cent adjustment (SOPA), the effective discount is much higher. For example, if the formal discount for sprinklers is 50 per cent and the SOPA for the industry is 200 per cent, then the rate for sprinklered premises turns out to be only 13⅓ per cent of that of unsprinklered premises.[37] Some typical examples showing the effects of sprinkler protection on rating are given here in Table 5.2. Similarly, in the US sprinkler protection is a common requirement under the HPR concept and rating discounts of 60, 70 or 80 per cent are common under the Analytic and other rating schedules.

Table 5.2

Some examples of the effects of sprinklers on premium rating

| Occupancy of risk | Rate quoted for actual risk (pounds per £100) | | Percentage reduction in rate |
|---|---|---|---|
| | Without sprinklers | With sprinklers | |
| Metalworking | 0·225 | 0·072 | 68 |
| Book warehouse | 0·788 | 0·07 | 91 |
| Glass warehouse | 1·8 | 0·25 | 86 |
| Clothing manufacture | 0·9 | 0·156 | 83 |
| Tannery | 2·1 | 0·288 | 86 |
| Miscellaneous food manufacture | 0·188 | 0·06 | 68 |
| Shopping centre | 0·155 | 0·06 | 48 |

Source: Supplied from the files of a large insurance broker.

An analysis of the size and development of the sprinkler market is made very difficult by the almost total absence of any collective data. One estimate that has been made suggests that in 1970 the national expenditure on sprinklers in the UK was of the order of £34 million, of which £25 million related to new installations and £9 million to maintenance of existing installations.[38] My own estimate for national expenditure on new installations for 1973 is £25 million, this being estimated from information given by some six installing firms on their own sales and their estimated market share. The apparent absence of growth between the years 1970 and 1973 probably reflects the problems of estimation rather than underlying stagnation; indeed, several firms gave verbal confirmation of modest though not spectacular growth. It therefore appears that for 1973 national expenditure on new installations was probably in the region of £25–32·5 million with perhaps another £11 million for the maintenance of existing installations.

Whilst this point estimate is rather crude, there is no available information showing the growth and development of the sprinkler market over time. However, comments made by firms do lend some support to the view that the fortunes of the sprinkler industry and the activities of insurers are closely linked. Several firms reported large increases in their orders for installations during two periods, the first being during 1965 and the second 1969. Significantly, the first of these periods coincided with the introduction of the SOPAs which caused sudden dramatic increases in the effective premium discounts for sprinkler installations. The second period coincided with an announcement changing the FOC rules for admissible installations to the so-called 29th edition rules which were only to apply to new installations and a period of grace was allowed before they came into operation. Since it was thought that the new rules would increase the cost of installations there was an apparent rush from insureds to get in under the older 28th edition rules.

The effect of premium reductions on sprinkler installations is to give a financial payback to the installations which is both substantial and easily measurable. Sprinkler installations can therefore be considered as investments which can be analysed, as can any other items of capital expenditure, on a cost-benefit basis. The results of such analysis often show sprinkler system as recouping very high rates of return.[39]

The response of insureds to the premium discounts for sprinkler installations was indicated by a survey conducted by the Central Fire Liaison Panel[40] of 85 firms, of whom 50 had recently installed some form of automatic fire defence system, 20 had considered such systems but had decided against installation, and a further 15 had not seriously considered such an investment. The results of the survey showed that insurance considerations played a major role in decisions to install automatic defence systems. Thus, for example, of the fifty companies with recently installed systems, 80 per cent suggested that savings in insurance premiums or threatened withdrawal of insurance cover had stimulated discussion in fire defence, and 86 per cent said that the insurer or broker had been involved in the discussions. For 96 per cent of the firms the installation attracted premium savings or was a condition of cover, and it appears that these factors, together with government capital grants, were the overriding factors in deciding to install the fire defence systems in the first place.

A further survey has been made of members of the Association of Insurance and Risk Managers in Industry and Commerce (AIRMIC).[41] This survey was conducted over a sample of insureds which is biased in favour of large firms; since the respondents were largely people with insurance backgrounds, they may also be particularly well informed about insurance rating structures and sympathetic to insurers' objectives. Thirty firms participated and of these all but one had either recently undertaken a review of fire protection for their existing building and plant or had a periodic procedure for such a review. In just over half of those cases, the insurer or broker had been involved in the review of fire protection and, in deciding what was the most important factor in making decisions on fire protection, the respondents were equally divided between employee safety, avoidance of business interruption and direct financial gain (i.e. premium concessions and capital grants). Others claimed that fire protection was company policy. One-third of the respondents had undertaken formal calculations of costs and benefits and a similar proportion argued that financial considerations were not an important factor in reaching a decision. The remainder, whilst admitting the importance of premium savings, government grants etc., had not formally calculated costs and benefits.

90 per cent of the firms responded on the question of fire protection for new premises which they had constructed or otherwise acquired. Insurance company/broker involvement in discussions was somewhat higher than for existing operations (72 per cent) but the most important factor in making a decision was again divided between employee safety (20 per cent), business interruption (35 per cent), direct financial gains (25 per cent) and company policy (20 per cent). 40 per cent had made a financial calculation of costs and benefits and 32 per cent suggested that financial considerations were unimportant: the remainder admitted the importance of financial motives but failed to quantify them.

The main difference between this survey and the BIA survey is that the former indicates that direct financial gain, particularly insurance premiums, or the threat of withdrawal of cover are probably the most important factors in deciding on automatic fire defence but that in the AIRMIC survey decisions on loss prevention are more broadly based. This reflects the spread of risk management techniques and a more comprehensive attitude towards risk in which insurance is considered alongside alternative methods of handling risk, namely risk retention and risk reduction. Whilst the role of insurance incentives is vitally important, the AIRMIC survey places it in the context of other important incentives (in particular, the avoidance of business interruption, which can be every bit as costly as direct damage yet can never be completely transferred under an insurance contract).

The cost effectiveness of installing a sprinkler system depends largely on three factors: the occupancy, the size of the establishment, and its eligibility for government capital investment grants. First, the premium saving from installing a sprinkler system is usually greater for high risk than for low risk occupancies. Secondly, there are scale economies from installing

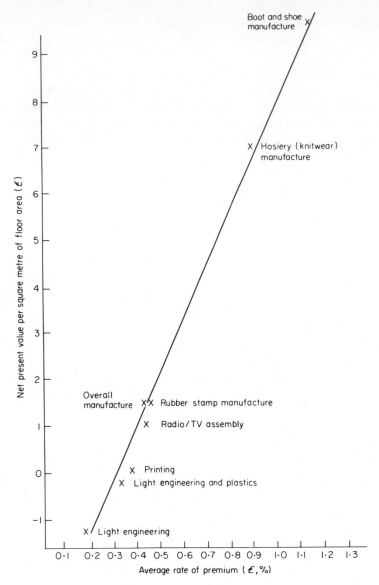

Fig. 5.4    Payback to sprinkler protection (risks in a grant assisted area of the UK)

systems in larger premises and the cost per unit of floor area protected diminishes with the size of the installation. Thirdly, in the UK, installations in development areas attract a capital grant so that these installations recoup a higher return on invested capital than corresponding ones outside the development areas.

The effect of these factors was considered in a series of case studies by N.D. Schofield,[42] and fig. 5.4 shows the results of one such set of studies. These results were obtained by considering the net present value (NPV) of an installation in a fairly small industrial building under alternative assumptions concerning the occupancy.[43] The size of the building was 778m², against an estimated average floor area for new sprinklered buildings of 4,552m²,[44] and the plant size, measured as the sum of the value of buildings and contents, varied between £114,000 for light engineering and engineering and plastics and £134,000 for other occupancies. Fig. 5.4 measures the net present value per square metre of floor area of each installation against the rate of insurance premium before the sprinkler system is installed. Since there are scale economies, it may be assumed that the NPV per square metre would be smaller for smaller plants and larger for larger plants. The critical plant size at which it becomes worthwhile to install a sprinkler system is therefore something slightly less than £134,000 for printing and something very considerably less than £134,000 for hosiery and boot and shoe manufacturers.[45]

In order to gain a rough idea of the response of individual insureds to premium incentives for sprinklers, a comparison is now made between the estimated percentage of establishments in selected industries with sprinkler protection and the estimated percentage which are above the critical size necessary to justify installation. A rough estimate of the distribution of establishments by value of building and contents is made by allocating the capital stock (building plus plant and machinery) for each industrial grouping on the following basis:

$$K \left[ \frac{Q_{ij}}{Q} \frac{1}{N_{ij}} \right]$$

where $K$ is the capital stock for the industry, $Q$ is the total output for the industry, $Q_{ij}$ is the total output of establishments employing between $i$ and $j$ persons, and $N_{ij}$ is the number of establishments employing between $i$ and $j$ persons.

The percentage of establishments in excess of £134,000 for the year 1973 is shown in column 1 of Table 5.3 for the groups (a) clothing and footwear, (b) electrical engineering and (c) paper printing and publishing. The industry groupings hosiery, footwear, and publishing are fairly representative in terms of fire hazard of these more general groupings and it appears safe to assume that the critical size to justify the installation is substantially below £134,000 for clothing and footwear, below £134,000 for electrical engineering and about £134,000 for publishing. Column 2 plots the estimated percentage of establishments with sprinklers in 1965. These percentages will be an overestimate since some establishments are only partly sprinklered.

Table 5.3

The incidence of sprinkler protection in selected industries

| Industry | Percentage of establishments above critical size for economic installation, 1973 | Percentage of establishments with sprinklers, 1965 |
|---|---|---|
| Clothing and footwear | 18+ | 29 |
| Electrical engineering | 72+ | 7 |
| Paper printing and publishing | 60 | 33 |

Note: Both columns relate to establishments which employ more than ten persons.
Source: (1) Census of Production, HMSO 1968.
(2) Annual Abstract of Statistics, HMSO 1973.
(3) National Accounts.
(4) G. Ramachandran, 'An enquiry into the frequency of sprinklered premises', Fire Research Station, note no.828, May 1970.


It has been separately estimated that since 1965 the number of sprinkler installations has been growing by 10–15 per cent annually[46] and though some of these will relate to existing establishments the large majority relate to new premises.[47] It seems unlikely, therefore, that the large differential between (a) the percentage of electrical engineering and publishing establishments which are sprinklered and (b) the percentage for which sprinklers could be justified on a NPV basis has been removed over this period. For clothing and footwear, on the other hand, the comparison between the rational level and the actual level is inconclusive. These results might be partly explained by assuming that individuals use somewhat higher rates of discount than that chosen by Schofield. Nevertheless, they do lend tentative support to the view that, whilst premium incentives for the installation of sprinklers are substantial, the response of insureds is somewhat dulled by a paucity of information on the subject.

# Notes

[1] British Insurance Association.

[2] Fire Protection Association.

[3] The ratio if direct to other costs is taken from A. Silcock, 'Protecting a building against fire – background to cost', *Architects' Journal*, 13 December 1967.

[4] These figures are based on analysis of insurance company returns to the Department of Trade and information supplied by the British Insurance Association.

[5] C. Arthur Williams, *Price Discrimination in Property and Liability Insurance*, University of Minnesota Press, Minneapolis 1959, p.31.

[6] Monopolies Commission, *Fire Insurance – Report on the Supply of Fire Insurance*, HMSO, London 1972, para.273.

[7] Monopolies Commission, op.cit., para.57.

[8] The FOC itself accepts the arbitrary nature of many of the subdivisions in the classification system. See A.A. Maclaren, 'The work of the FOC', *Journal of the Chartered Insurance Institute*, vol.70, 1973, p.17.

[9] See K.R. Benn, 'Sprinkler discounts: the hit or miss of fire protection', *Policyholder*, vol.89, 24 December 1971, pp.2281–2.

[10] See R.L. Carter and N.A. Doherty, 'Tariff control and the public interest – report on British fire insurance', *Journal of Risk and Insurance*, September 1974, p.494.

[11] These issues are discussed in Carter and Doherty, op.cit.

[12] Monopolies Commission, op.cit., para.338.

[13] If pure premiums are correctly calculated, the use of target loss ratios will produce proportionate loadings for each insured. However, if the figure for expected claims used by the insurers differs from its true value, then the loading factor for any given insured may well be random.

[14] Monopolies Commission, op.cit., para.342.

[15] Monopolies Commission, op.cit., para.144.

[16] Monopolies Commission, op.cit., Appendix B.

[17] A.F. Dean, *The Analytic System for the Measurement of Fire Hazards*. The analytic schedule bears similarities to the earlier Universal Mercantile System published in 1892.

[18] T.C. Allen and R.M. Duval, *Property Insurance Rating; A Plea for Change*, American Society of Insurance Management, New York 1973, p.41.

[19] C. Arthur Williams, op.cit., p.91.

[20] T.C. Allen and R.M. Duval, op.cit.

[21] See M.R. Green, *Risk and Insurance*, 2nd ed., South Western

Publishing Co., Cincinnati 1968, pp.726–7.

[22] C. Arthur Williams, op.cit., p.91.

[23] See 'The Insurance Industry', Antitrust and Monopoly Committee on the Judiciary, US Senate, 86th Congress, US Government Printing Office, Washington DC 1960, pp.240 ff.

[24] This conclusion is reached by R.J. Hensley in *Competition, Regulation and the Public Interest in Non-Life Insurance*, University of California Press, Berkeley 1962.

[25] David R. Klock, 'Competitive rating laws and insurer conduct', *Journal of Risk and Insurance*, vol.39, December 1972; and C. Arthur Williams and Andrew F. Whitman, 'Open competition rating laws and price competition', *Journal of Risk and Insurance*, vol.40, December 1973.

[26] Monopolies Commission, op.cit., para.378.

[27] Ibid., para.381.

[28] However, the Monopolies Commission has not thought it advisable to make collective pools of statistics obligatory should the tariff be abolished. (Monopolies Commission, op.cit., para.396.)

[29] These points are developed by K.I. Jordan in *Fortuity Indemnity and Risk Control. The Philosophy of Fire Insurance and its Social and Economic Functions in the post-Holroyd era*, on file, Chartered Insurance Institute Library, London 1973. See also 'Pity the poor surveyor', *Post Magazine and Insurance Monitor*, 23 March 1972.

[30] J. Finley Lee, 'The competitive role of the Associated Factory Mutuals', *Journal of Risk Insurance*, vol.36, 1969, p.414.

[31] Estimates for one very large UK insurer reveal that 3·2 per cent of fire premium income is accounted for by surveying expenses. Comparative figures for liability and burglary insurance for the same insurer are 0·6 per cent and 6·1 per cent. For another leading insurer the ratio for fire surveying was 1·5 per cent of premium income.

[32] J.I.H. Meier, 'Service to industry', paper presented to the Annual Conference of the Chartered Insurance Institute, 1973.

[33] Ibid.

[34] Allen and Duval, op.cit., p.157.

[35] 'The why's and wherefore's of sprinkler protection', *FPA Journal*, no.65.

[36] *United Kingdom Fire and Loss Statistics*, Department of the Environment and Fire Offices Committee, 1971, JFRO Table 17a. These figures relate to fires attended by brigades and may not be strictly comparable with the unknown sources of the FPA data.

[37] If $x$ is the initial rate of premium, then the premium for unsprink-

lered risks is $x \times 0\cdot5 \times 0\cdot8 = 0\cdot4x$. For sprinklered premises the rate is $x + 2x = 3x$, i.e. nearly eight times the rate for unsprinklered risks.

[38] G. Ramachandran, 'National expenditure on sprinkler installations', Fire Research Station, note no.906, December 1971.

[39] N.D. Schofield, 'An Economic Appraisal of Aspects of Automatic Fire Defence', M.Phil. thesis, University of Aston; see also N.D. Schofield, Case Study no.3 in *Handbook of Risk Management* (ed. Carter and Doherty), Kluwer Harrap, London 1974.

[40] 'Company attitudes to installation of automatic fire prevention/detection systems', unpublished survey prepared for the Central Fire Liaison Panel.

[41] Undertaken for this study.

[42] N.D. Schofield, op.cit.

[43] The main benefits identified in the calculations were premium savings on material damage and consequential loss premiums and capital grants (the costs being installation and maintenance costs). Costs and benefits were specified in constant prices and discounted at 5 per cent.

[44] G. Ramachandran, op.cit.

[45] The critical value identifies an optimal level for the individual but not a social optimum, since the interaction of premium reductions and capital grants need not reflect the effective reduction in the expected value of losses.

[46] G. Ramachandran, op.cit.

[47] Information supplied by several installers.

# 6 Motor insurance pricing and loss prevention

The social cost of road accidents can be very largely measured in terms of injuries and lives lost. These costs do impose serious problems of valuation, yet, even using the minimum estimates, the total cost of road accidents in Great Britain in 1973 including loss of life, medical treatment, loss of output and damage to property was estimated at £615 million.[1] This figure takes no account of the pain, suffering and grief of the victims and their relatives.

The potential influence of insurance on this figure is high since insurance protection is a legal prerequisite of the use of a motor vehicle and also affords financial freedom from the very high liabilities which may be incurred in road accidents. This chapter therefore examines the role of insurance incentives in determining or influencing vehicle ownership and usage and driver behaviour.

## Some broad comparisons between the UK fire and motor insurance markets

The present structure of the motor market is summarised in Table 6.1 in terms of the percentages of market premium income controlled by the largest insurers. These concentration ratios are compared with those for the fire market. This comparison understates the differences in monopolistic control between the two markets since, as was seen in the previous chapter, the FOC exercises a large degree of centralised control over about 63 per cent of the fire market, whereas no such cartel exists in the motor market. However, the present structure of the motor market is the product of a rapid and traumatic evolution.

In the mid-fifties there existed broad similarities between the UK fire insurance market and the UK motor insurance market. Like the fire market, the motor market was dominated by a tariff organisation, the Accident Offices Association (AOA), which controlled about two-thirds of the premium income in the motor market and to which most of the large offices belonged. Offices which belonged to the FOC were required by the rules of the Committee to belong to the AOA if they also conducted

## Table 6.1

### Concentration in the UK fire and motor insurance markets, 1972

|  | Motor (%) | Fire (%) |
|---|---|---|
| Market share of: |  |  |
| Top company | 10·6 | 13 |
| Top five companies | 35·4 | 58 |
| Top nine companies | 51·1 | 74 |

Source: Monopolies Commission Report, company returns and Lloyd's published figures.

accident business. Lloyd's were relatively more important in the motor than in the fire insurance market, accounting for about half of the non-tariff premium income. However, there were certain technical and market features which made the structure of the motor market less stable than the fire market and the period from the mid-Fifties to the present has seen drastic structural changes culminating in the break-up of the tariff on 1 January 1969.

Competition has certainly been more vigorous in the motor insurance market than in fire insurance and this is in large part due to differences in the nature of the product involved. In the first place, a typical fire insurer's portfolio will contain far fewer independent units of exposure than the typical motor portfolio and, in addition, the individual risks in the fire portfolio will tend to exhibit far more variability in their loss experience than the motor risks. The implication is that a motor portfolio is much more amenable to statistical analysis and that the collective experience of a motor portfolio is much more relevant to the rating of the individual risk than is the case in fire insurance.[2]

The second technical difference between fire and motor insurance also relates to the credibility of statistical data. Because of differences in the relative frequency of fire and motor losses of the individual insured, it is usually much easier to draw inferences from past experience about the degree of innate risk for a motor insurance proposal than it is for a fire proposal. For this reason, motor underwriters have formally included experience rating in their rating structures and it is this feature that has played a key role in the development of the motor insurance market in the 1960s and into the 1970s.

## The United Kingdom motor insurance market – historical development

The historical development of the UK motor insurance market provides a good illustration of the model of selective competition developed in earlier chapters. In particular, it shows how competitive pressures have led to more efficient discriminating rating structures.

The AOA tariff rating system provides the model for many systems currently in use. The portfolio was subdivided into cells on the basis of engine size, value of vehicle, garage area and class of use. Superimposed on this was a scale of no-claims discount (NCD) and further flexibility was introduced by the provision for special rating on application to the AOA, though this facility was used for relatively few risks.[3] As in the fire tariff, the agreement was to uphold minimum rates of premium, though members were free to load above the tariff subject only to the sanction of market demand.

Throughout its later years the AOA share of the market declined rapidly. Whereas in the mid-Fifties the tariff share was about two-thirds of the market premium income, at the time immediately preceding its collapse at the beginning of 1969 this share had fallen to one-third. The swing of business away from the tariff bloc may be seen as a consequence of both the system of minimum pricing and the rigidity of the tariff structure.[4] Apart from the very small companies, the non-tariff insurers had largely enjoyed lower ratios of commission plus expenses to premium income than the tariff companies and were consequently able to attract business across the whole range of good to bad drivers by offering lower basic premiums.[5] However, since the non-tariff NCD scales were more generous, the appeal of the non-tariff market was strongest for those with several years claim-free driving. In this way, the non-tariff insurers were able to practise selective competition against the tariff bloc since the tariff share was not only declining, but was also being left with the worst business.

The tactics of the non-tariff bloc in attracting low risk drivers is in evidence in the Consumer Association's report of 1966[6] which shows that many of the non-tariff insurers were offering the same basic premium as the tariff or were discounting the tariff premium at a constant sum or percentage.[7] The differences in the premiums between tariff and non-tariff are much more marked when compared net of NCD.[8] In addition, the non-tariff companies reinforced premium incentives with advertising campaigns aimed at the careful driver and also with selective use of the 'underwriter's nose' (i.e. underwriting by hunch and experience rather than by reference to objective loss data).[9]

The consequence of the differences in NCD scales was a leapfrogging process in which the AOA changed its NCD rules and increased its scale in order to win back the good drivers. However, this only succeeded in provoking further retaliatory action from the non-tariff insurers who simply increased their own NCD scales. Thus the low risk business continued to drift away from the tariff market until the tariff insurers finally rid themselves of the cartel restrictions by dissolving the tariff in 1969.

The immediate reaction to the ending of the tariff was a mad scramble for business. The tariff had prevented many of the larger companies from competing for the good drivers. The effect of the newly found freedom and the uncertainty which followed the disappearance of a price leader was a 'free for all' in rate cutting. The scene was aptly described by the chairman of the Vehicle and General in his annual report for 1968: '. . . if one may judge from the rates being quoted by some of the former tariff companies, their underwriters appear to have been replaced by their marketing advisers'.[10]

The competitive struggle which erupted in 1969 was short-lived. During the last years of the tariff profit margins had been low and, in retrospect, it seems clear that the exercise conducted by the ex-tariff offices of cutting their base rates and simultaneously increasing their NCD scales could only have been temporary. The exercise may simply have been one of re-establishing the consumer loyalties of the good drivers. However, the coincidence of a massive increase in claims costs, due both to an increase in the number of claims and to inflation, made rate increases inevitable. Since then the market has witnessed frequent and substantial rounds of price increases.

Writing in 1971, Professor G. Clayton said that it was '. . . obviously premature to make a realistic assessment of the competitive structure which has emerged since the situation is extremely fluid. But one thing is certain, it [the breakup of the tariff] has ushered in an era of innovation and experimentation with profound effects on the entire range of the industry's activities'.[11] Certainly, the willingness to experiment is in evidence in the Consumer Association's report of 1969.[12] The ninety-nine companies and Lloyd's syndicates listed there between them account for fifty-four different types of NCD systems and the thirteen ex-tariff companies shown produce ten different bonus systems. The willingness to experiment with new NCD systems reflects an attempt on the part of the ex-tariff companies to win back the low risk business. However, a subsequent Consumer Association report in 1972[13] reflects increased stability in the market. Instead of quoting long lists of rates for each insurer, this report is able to summarise by giving a typical rating scheme together with a typical form and scale of NCD. This may be seen as a cautionary reaction to the violent competition of the previous year or so but it also reflects the benefits of collective statistics. Innovation had ceased to be a marketing gimmick and had become more solidly based on actuarial analysis.

## The allocation of claims costs between insureds

In order to see whether motor insurers achieve an efficient allocation of claims costs between insureds, it is necessary to examine the selection of factors used for rating, the role of the so-called 'special policies' and the statistical facilities for quantifying the effects of the various rating factors. (The effect of NCD structures is considered later in the chapter.)

The old tariff rating structure was severely criticised for concentrating on the wrong rating factors, or at least ignoring the more important ones. A report commissioned by the industry, the McKinsey Report, suggested that the tariff had concentrated on car characteristics rather than the more important driver characteristics. In particular, the age of the driver, which was a highly relevant and easily administered variable, was largely over-looked. Furthermore, whilst the motor tariff was much more firmly based on statistical material than was the fire tariff,[14] the McKinsey Report and the train of events leading to the break-up of the tariff suggest that the use of statistics did not go far enough.

The performance of the industry during the 1969 price war certainly had a sobering effect. During the tariff period the non-tariff insurers had been able to expand their share of the market with ease but, with the tariff gone and its members free to compete, their advantage was removed and the good business began to swing back to the ex-tariff companies. If the 1969 price war did not spell out the dangers of inadequate underwriting, then the collapse of the Vehicle and General in 1971 must certainly have done so.[15] The need for more scientific rate making was also underlined by the effects of accelerating inflation on reserve funds. The so-called 'long tail' of motoring third party claims meant that many claims were being paid several years after the corresponding premiums had been received; with increasing prices the final value of unreported and outstanding claims was, in many cases, turning out to be much larger than the amounts reserved. These factors, together with the BIA's attempts to provide for the collec-tivisation of statistics, have undoubtedly improved the discriminatory power of rating systems.

## Selection of rating factors

Apart from NCD, the principle rating factors which had been used in the tariff and which have continued in general use after its break-up are usage, vehicle characteristics and garage area. Since these factors are thought to explain the distribution of accidents it may also be assumed that as these factors change so too will their frequency. But these factors are not easily manipulated. It requires a change in car or, even more drastically, a change of job or moving to a new home in a new town to move between different risk categories. Differences in insurance premiums may therefore be a relatively small item in the table of costs and benefits which flow from the change and, as such, they are unlikely to have much influence on decisions.[16] If we are concerned with the use of insurance as a policy variable with which to manipulate accident frequencies, then it will certainly prove ineffective. However, if we are trying to find the correct level of resources to be allocated to accident prevention, then this does not matter. If accident costs are a relatively small item in the table of costs and benefits of adjustment it would be economically inefficient to treat them otherwise. What is important is that insurance premiums do not distort these costs, and in this context statistical verification becomes important. However, decisions are made at the margin and a relatively small item may tip the balance.

Another feature of adjustments in car ownership, usage or garage location is that they involve sizeable transaction costs. If a certain make of car is associated with a particularly bad accident record, then the insurers, depending on the credibility of the evidence, may well wish to adjust their premiums for that make of car. Some owners may then feel that the advantages of having that make of vehicle are outweighed by the increased insurance premiums but, nevertheless, will not change cars because the transaction costs are too high. In time, other factors such as age, reliability, prestige etc., will reinforce the pressure to change the vehicle and at this stage insurance premiums may be an important determinant of the choice of new car. There can be little doubt, for example, that high insurance premiums have curbed the population of high performance sports cars over the last few years, but adjustments such as these tend to occur over relatively long time periods.

The close association between age and loss frequency has been clear for some time, but, in spite of the McKinsey recommendation, it was not taken up by the tariff as a primary rating factor. Although many companies had been penalising young drivers, usually by means of increased excesses or arbitrary premium loadings, the use of age as a rating factor was unsystematic and some companies ignored it altogether. The initiative was taken up by a non-tariff company, the Midland Northern and Scottish, which produced a rating system based almost entirely on the age of the policyholder, other factors being regulated by means of a system of quotas and excesses. Although, through its relative neglect of other factors, selective competition led to the downfall of the MN & S,[17] the use of age alongside other rating factors has now become widely established. The use of age has been further encouraged by the Motor Risk Statistics Bureau (MRSB) which provides a collective analysis of the returns of many of the larger companies. The collation associates claims frequencies with factors such as type and age of vehicle, garage area and age of driver.[18] In this climate, any company which ignores age as a rating factor will run the risk of overloading its portfolio with young high risk drivers and will suffer a corresponding deterioration in its loss experience.

The relevance of age related premiums for loss prevention may seem a little obscure since, apart from making fraudulent declarations to the insurance company, the insured cannot manipulate his age to enter a lower risk category. However, this does not mean that age related premiums are purely a matter of equity and balanced underwriting since, in penalising young drivers, they reinforce the incentives for careful and limited driving contained in the NCD system. It may well be that it is the young driver who has most need of incentives to careful driving. If his basic premium is high, then his potential gain from a proportional NCD system is very much greater than that of the middle-aged driver whose basic premium is lower and who is much more likely to drive carefully for reasons of maturity, common prudence and social responsibility. In addition, the use of age related premiums may effectively exclude some drivers in certain high risk age groups from cover altogether or may force them to participate in the risk in order to avoid the prohibitive costs of comprehensive cover.

Another factor which is assumed to be closely associated with accident frequency is mileage driven. However, apart from the somewhat loose association between mileage and the use classification, this factor has traditionally been ignored, largely because of difficulties of verification. One exception is a 'special' policy[19] which relies to some extent on mileage in limiting cover to those whose annual mileage does not exceed a given figure. A more radical approach has been introduced by another company, the Guardian Royal Exchange, which has apparently found that a more successful proxy for mileage than usage is to base premiums on commuting distances. Should this approach result in selection favourable to the company, it seems likely that others will adopt the practice.

The general omission of mileage as a rating factor may have serious implications for loss prevention since it focusses more directly than other rating factors on marginal adjustment. 'The basic difficulty is that the insurance premium appears to the automobile owner almost entirely as part of the fixed cost of owning a car.'[20] The result is that the additional exposure to risk from more intensive use of a car (as opposed to the use of public transport or not making trips at all) is not brought to bear in decisionmaking. Whilst a mileage related premium does encounter administrative problems, it is not clear whether these are insuperable. Whilst there are problems of honesty in making declarations to the insurer, these are not necessarily more acute than with other insurance contracts where the principle of 'utmost good faith' also applies. However, a more radical alternative which has been suggested is the levy of an insurance tax on petrol.[21] Such a scheme would not encounter the problems of good faith and would be cheap and simple to administer. However, it does carry the implication, whether desirable or not, that the insurance function would be transferred from the private to the state sector.

## Special policies

Perhaps the main vehicle for innovation in the period following the collapse of the tariff has been the introduction of the so-called 'special' policies. The features common to most of these policies are that they discourage the young, the inexperienced and the owners of powerful cars.[22] Furthermore, admission to these special schemes is usually on the basis of a good driving record as evidenced by attaining a minimum point on the NCD scale. The effect of these special policies on loss prevention is unclear. Their particular attraction is that they offer low premiums and/or generous cover for a restricted class of low risk drivers. Thus the desire to enter such a scheme provides an incentive for careful driving. However, part of the appeal is that most of the schemes are not subject to NCD and, consequently, the incentives for careful and limited driving which are conveyed through the bonus structure are lost.

## The use of statistics

The second function of the AOA, the collection and assembly of statistics, has also attracted criticism and even before the collapse of the tariff a new body, the Motor Risk Statistics Bureau, had been formed by the BIA to assemble loss statistics from the industry. The MRSB was established in 1967, largely on the recommendation of the McKinsey Report, and, with the collapse of the tariff, it now plays a crucial role in the provision of information upon which individual companies base their premiums.[23]

The MRSB basically performs two functions. First, it assembles claims information from companies which is aggregated and made available to all members. In practice, information is only obtained from companies which are able to process their information on a computer and present it to the MRSB in a suitably coded form. This limits returns to the larger companies but the number of offices participating appears to be increasing. All member companies, whether they submit claims information or not, receive a quarterly analysis of the collective results. This collective information is classified according to four usage groups – year and make of vehicle, age of policyholder, garage area, and whether cover is comprehensive or not. There are problems of comparability of data, particularly since offices differ in the forms of cover they offer and in their treatment of claims, but, nevertheless, it is felt that such collective statistics produce a more credible base for rating than the statistics of an individual office. This is particularly important for the small company whose portfolio is unlikely to provide a reliable rating guide.

On the one hand, the provision of collective information serves as a reminder to firms of the dangers of ignoring the statistical associations revealed by MRSB data in their rating structures. In this respect the MRSB data ensure a certain uniformity in rating structures. On the other hand, the provision of collective statistics has given companies a certain independence of action in pricing motor risks. With the collapse of the tariff a price leadership situation disappeared. Without collective rating, many small and medium-sized companies would have been forced to copy the rating structures of their larger competitors rather than rely on producing somewhat shaky rates from their own statistics. In the event, no clear situation of price leadership has emerged.

The first major function of the MRSB is thus to make a common body of statistical information available to its members. Its second function is to provide private information to participating companies. In addition to collective statistics, member companies making returns are provided with an analysis of their own rating areas and car groups. This duality of functions thus reflects a conflict of interests. The benefit of collective information is that it is more reliable than that available to an individual company and it can be produced at lower unit cost. The reliable basic statistical information is spread throughout the market. The companies with most to gain are the smaller companies. On the other hand, a system in which information is made public removes the incentive for innovation since it is privity of information which enables the innovating firm to make monopoly profits. The approach of the MRSB reflects a compromise. The bait for the larger companies (or those making returns) is that they are encouraged to experiment with new car and area groupings and that the MRSB respects the competitive advantages which this may bring. Furthermore, companies are not compelled to submit their statistics to the MRSB nor does submission and analysis by the MRSB preclude analysis by the companies themselves, and some companies also have their own staff researching on improved ways of explaining the distribution of claims.

It is not only important that information is available to insurers to facilitate their rating, but also that information is available to insureds in a form that signals the cost implications of alternative choices which are available at the time the decision is made. It is probably safe to assume that the vast majority of insureds have no detailed knowledge of premium rating structures due both to the complexity of these structures and the traditional closeness of insurers about the details of their operations. In most cases, the only figure which the proposer knows is the quotation which has been given to him by one or a number of insurers or brokers for a vehicle which has already been purchased. Probably the only details he has of the rating scheme is the NCD scale which, as stated elsewhere in this chapter, conveys no information about specific actions which will affect his accident expectancy. One of the outcomes of the collectivisation of statistics is that it has led to a fair degree of standardisation in the breakdown of rateable factors. The MRSB has a seven category breakdown of cars and this breakdown, or something very similar, has been adopted by the majority of the large insurers. This feature has enabled outside organisations, such as consumer organisations, driving organisations, motor magazines and manufacturers themselves, to classify vehicles in terms of their insurance rating category. In this way, information on insurance rating is often brought to the attention of the prospective purchaser at the time he is deciding which type of car to purchase.

Insurers themselves have generally failed to convey specific information of this type to the public. Whilst it may be argued that incentives for loss prevention have improved with greater discrimination in premium structures, this is to little avail if these incentives are not backed up by information which can be used at the time the insured makes decisions concerning safety. This point is developed further by example. It is usual in motor policies to include a clause concerning the roadworthiness of the vehicle. If this condition is not fulfilled, the insurer can avoid liability. However, the clause does not contain any detailed information of what should be done to keep insurance cover intact; thus it may not be as likely to induce behavioural change as an alternative clause requiring that the insured shall have the vehicle regularly serviced, maintain tyres to appropriate pressure and depth of tread, maintain lighting system in good order etc. There are one or two schemes in operation which do latch on to specific safety features: some cancel own damage cover in the event of drunken driving, another extends personal accident benefits if a seat belt is worn and another contains a special discount for safety wheels. But this type of approach is the exception rather than the rule. If the information collated for premium rating is to be used efficiently in decisions concerning safety and loss prevention, then more attention is needed in the transmission of this information to the insuring public.

Finally, an example of response to specific information on safety is given, and though this example does not involve the insurance sector, it does highlight the importance of the transmission of information. Seat belts, if properly worn, can reduce the probability of serious injury by up to 50 per cent.[24] In 1972 the British government devoted considerable resources to television campaigns aimed at raising the level of seat belt wearing. Roadside observations in the three areas where the campaign was

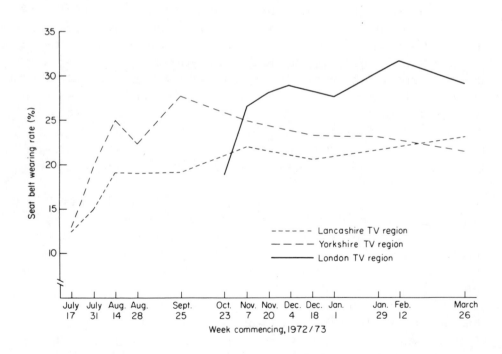

Fig. 6.1   Level of seat belt wearing amongst front seat occupants of cars and light vans with seat belts fitted, 1972/73

conducted show the trends illustrated in Fig. 6.1. Although it is not known whether these improvements will be sustained in the long term, certainly the short term response is quite significant.

## The allocation of expenses between insureds

As with fire insurance, it is difficult to obtain estimates of the ratio of claims to premiums since insurance publicity material does not include this statistic nor do official statistics show claims on a UK basis. However, information is available on a company basis in returns made to the Department of Trade under the Insurance Companies Acts. For the top ten companies, which account for over half the market premium income, the weighted average ratio of claims paid and outstanding incurred within the year to premiums earned within the year was 65·9 per cent for 1972 and 64·3 per cent for 1973.[25] Claims ratios do tend to fluctuate from year to year and, whilst companies confirmed that they were significantly higher in the years 1969 to 1971, many suggested that ratios of the order of 65 per cent were about the long term norm.

The differential between claims and premiums has not been used to support high levels of profit, and in several years, particularly those after the break-up of the tariff, substantial underwriting losses were made. The figures below, provided by the British Insurance Association, show home underwriting profit or loss as a percentage of premiums for the period 1963–73. (The figures marked by an asterisk include the Republic of Eire.)

| 1963 | 1964 | 1965 | 1966 | 1967 | 1968 | 1969 | 1970 | 1971 | 1972 | 1973 |
|------|------|------|------|------|------|------|------|------|------|------|
| −2·8* | 1·4* | −2·1* | 0·7* | 0·6* | 1·3 | −7·3 | −14·5 | −8·6 | −0·8 | 2·7 |

Of the residual, about 10 per cent of premiums goes to commission, though the percentage is somewhat higher for Lloyd's and some companies where much of the underwriting and administrative work is undertaken by the broker, and internal expenses account for the rest.

The structure of premium loading is also important and here practice differs between companies. Whilst some companies suggested that expenses were allocated on a proportionate basis, others said they attempted a more efficient allocation of the form

$$P = a_1 C + a_2 P + a_3$$

where $P$ is the premium, $C$ is the expected claims cost, $a_1$ and $a_2$ are the proportions of expenses which might be appropriately related to claims and premiums respectively, and $a_3$ is expenses which are independent of claims and premiums.[26] This form of loading is of the combination form referred to in chapter 3. If decisions on loss prevention are made on a purely financial basis, the effect of insurance may be expected to increase loss prevention expenditure, but, on the wider allocative criteria, this form of loading appears to be preferable to the simple proportionate loading.

## No claims discount schemes and loss prevention

One of the ironies of the McKinsey Report was that it simultaneously criticised the tariff for its neglect of driver characteristics yet recommended discontinuing the only element of the premium structure which had taken these features into account, namely the NCD. After discounting other factors such as engine capacity, use and garage area which could be handled very easily for statistical purposes, much of the residual variation was assumed to reflect driver characteristics and to be reflected in the accident record. In the event, NCD has taken on an increased importance as it now explains to a much larger extent than in pre-McKinsey days the variation in premiums between different insureds.

The potency of experience rating schemes in deterring claims can be seen by considering a fairly representative scheme. Although NCD schemes in current use do vary, it is possible to identify one which is fairly typical.[27] For each claim-free year, the discount is increased one point along the scale: zero; 30 per cent; 40 per cent; 50 per cent; 60 per cent. With one claim in a period of insurance the insured jumps back two places but with more than one claim in the year the insured returns to zero. The opportunity cost of lodging a claim is shown as the accumulated discount lost in future years expressed as a percentage of the basic premium as in Table 6.2. These totals take no account of the timing of the future increased premium and the figures in the third row have been adjusted to allow for time preference at a rate of 10 per cent. The striking thing about this scale is that it penalises people in the middle of the scale more than people at the bottom or at the top. In contrast, under the types of discount schemes which were common a decade ago (in particular, the pre-1966 tariff scheme) the insured forfeited all discount with a single claim regardless of his position on the scale at the time of loss. Schemes of this form tend to increase the penalty for lodging a claim as the insured moves up the scale.

Table 6.2

Cumulative discount lost after lodging one claim

| | Percentage of basic premium | | | | |
|---|---|---|---|---|---|
| Discount in year of accident | 60 | 50 | 40 | 30 | 0 |
| Accumulated discount foregone | 30 | 60 | 110 | 90 | 60 |
| Accumulated discount foregone (time preference rate = 10 per cent) | 26·1 | 50·5 | 90·5 | 73·4 | 49·0 |

The value and limitations of NCD in providing appropriate incentives for loss prevention can best be understood by comparison with other rating factors. It has been suggested that, in basing premiums on factors such as usage, vehicle characteristics and garage area, the premium appears as part of the fixed cost of owning a vehicle. These specific incentives provide no sanction on how the insured drives or how much he drives. It may well be that accident frequencies are every bit as sensitive to changes in driving habits and mileage driven as to the specific factors identified in the rating structure. The generalised incentives of the NCD scheme do provide a system of rewards for careful and limited driving, in fact they go further in providing some incentive to do absolutely anything which would reduce the probability of an accident and therefore a claim. In this way, NCD compensates for the specific deficiencies which arise either because some accident relevant features have not been identified in the rating structure, or because they have been given insufficient weighting. The point is made graphically in a comment on American rating systems: 'The nineteen year old, male, unmarried car owner can drive with the skill of a Rickenbacker and the caution of an Aunt Matilda without this having any effect on his high rate classification. In a sense it is precisely the class of driver which most needs the incentive for which the system provides the least incentive, in that his rate is already so high it can hardly go much further.'[28] The NCD scheme provides this type of incentive.

It was said of the specific rating factors that, whilst changes in these factors may affect accident frequencies, the costs of manipulating these factors are high. The economic costs of changes in driving habits may be quite low. True, slower driving necessarily implies longer travelling time[29] but, on the other hand, greater caution can often be exercised with relatively little loss of time and offsetting savings in wear and tear and fuel consumption. However, this stress on economic costs overemphasises the ease with which driving habits can be changed, since, as is stressed in the next chapter, driving habits are rooted in personality and changes here are not so responsive to rational financial controls.

A second limitation of the value of NCD systems is that they do not convey specific directions to the insured on how he might reduce his premium. It has been argued that one of the principal ways in which insurance can reduce losses is by transmitting information on the probabilities and consequences of loss. It follows that the generalised incentives of NCD are somewhat less effective in inducing behavioural change than rewards and penalties which result from specific actions of the insured. Using this argument, the NCD becomes something of a longstop. If rating schemes are to be evaluated in terms of risk discrimination then the use of NCD is a second best solution. This is not intended as a criticism of the use of NCD since second best solutions may be considered optimal where alternatives are not available. Some of the accident relevant features may be behavioural propensities which cannot be picked up in the general screening of insurance proposals since they only become known when accidents occur. Other features may be more easily identified but evidence is not very significant or may be too costly to acquire. In these cases, NCD might minimise the allocative distortion on the loss prevention market which is caused by the presence of insurance.

The efficiency with which NCD schemes compensate for deficiencies in the specific rating factors is now examined in more detail. Suppose that within a portfolio it is possible to isolate a group of drivers who are identical in terms of age, type of car, usage, occupation and garage area. Suppose further that 75 per cent of these drivers do not drive an excessive number of miles and drive carefully. Each of these drivers has an expected probability of an accident, or more correctly of a claim, of 0·1 in any one year. The remaining 25 per cent drive a greater mileage and with less care and have a probability of claim in any one year of 0·25. Since it is apparently borne out empirically that the expected size of claim is fairly constant in each risk group,[30] then the high risk group will have an expected claim cost equal to two and a half times that of the low risk group. However, as Johnson and Hey[31] point out in developing this example, the high risk group will pay only one-seventh more in premiums over the first ten years of insurance than the low risk group, given the fairly typical NCD structure outlined earlier in this chapter.

This example suggests that NCD schemes are relatively inefficient instruments for separating insureds according to the respective degrees of risk they each impose upon the insurance fund. It appears that the insured's position on the NCD scale is determined as much by chance as by inherent loss characteristics. However, the example does oversimplify. Other examples can be constructed to show that the relationship between differences in premiums payable and differences in loss probabilities varies according to which general order of loss probabilities is chosen in order to make the comparison. Furthermore, in practical situations motor insurers are faced with a continuous range of driving skills and loss probabilities rather than a dichotomous portfolio as used in the example. An alternative approach is to measure the sensitivity of premium changes brought about by movements along an NCD scale to changes in the expected value of loss. This approach is built on the proposition that changes in loss probability are reflected in loss experience. A measure designed to test the efficiency of NCD systems, and therefore of the incentives they provide for loss prevention, is provided by Loimaranta.[32]

The efficiency of an NCD scheme is defined as the responsiveness of changes in the premium payable to changes in the number of claims per year. More formally, the efficiency coefficient $\eta$ is defined as:

$$\eta = \frac{\lambda}{b} \cdot \frac{db}{d\lambda} = \frac{d \log b}{d \log \lambda}$$

where $b$ is the premium per period, and $\lambda$ is the expected number of claims.[33] Since it is assumed that the mean value of claims is constant in each risk group, the expected claims cost is proportional to the expected number of claims. An efficiency measure of unity therefore suggests that premium and claims bear a constant proportional relationship and that an $x$ per cent change in claims cost will result in an $x$ per cent change in premiums. Such a system is clearly efficient. Inefficient systems display values of $\eta$ less than unity, ie the NCD scheme is insensitive to changes in the expected number of claims and overefficient schemes are signified by values of $\eta$ in excess of unity. The techniques for calculating values for $\eta$ are described by Loimaranta[34] and a computer programme was written to perform the necessary calculations.[35]

The efficiency measure for an NCD scheme is not constant over different risk groups: the measure varies over the range of the expected number of claims. This feature is seen in Fig. 6.2: the NCD scheme operated by the tariff prior to 1966 was most efficient for that subgroup of the portfolio which had an expected claim frequency in the region of 0·3 to 0·4 claims per year. The scheme was less efficient for drivers with higher and lower loss probabilities.

Fig. 6.2 shows the effect of competitive pressures on the discriminatory

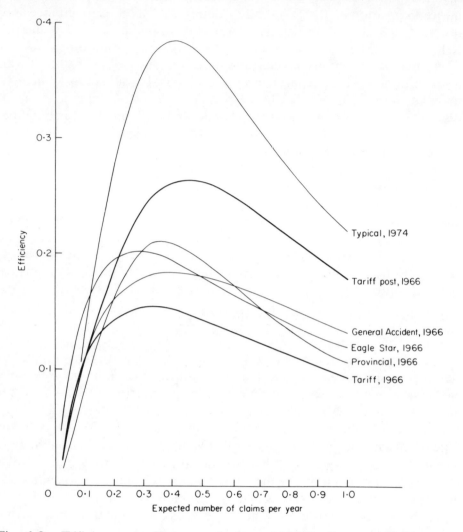

Fig. 6.2   Efficiency coefficients of selected NCD schemes: development over time

power of motor rating structures. It was suggested that the demise of the tariff was largely due to selective competition exercised by independent insurers by manipulation of their NCD schemes. Here it can clearly be seen that the NCD systems being operated by a sample of four of the largest independent offices in 1966 tended to be more efficient over most of their range than the tariff scheme. Retaliation by the tariff produced a new scheme which was in turn more efficient over most of its range than most of the competing schemes.[36] The competitive 'free for all' which followed the break-up of the tariff has produced still more efficient schemes as illustrated by the representative scheme described above.

Although the developments of the last decade have produced NCD schemes of increasing efficiency, and have therefore improved incentives for more careful driving, there is no evidence that this process has worn itself out. Fig. 6.3 measures the efficiency of a sample of schemes currently in operation: the sample accounts for over 60 per cent of the UK motor market as measured by premium income and includes the top ten companies and a sample of other insurers. The figure shows a cluster of insurers who operate schemes which differ little in either the scale of discounts or in the rules which prescribe movement between different points on the scale. However, three of the companies – the Guardian Royal Exchange (the second largest motor underwriter excluding Lloyd's), the Co-op (the fifth largest) and the Cornhill (the twelfth largest) – operate schemes which differ markedly from the others. These three schemes all reach higher peaks of efficiency than the cluster. Two of them, the GRE and the Cornhill, tend to be more efficient in adjusting premiums to expected claims costs for the low risk groups than the cluster but less efficient for the high risk groups. The Co-op scheme, however, is no less efficient than the cluster for the low risk groups and considerably more efficient for the high risk groups. Although other aspects of premium structures will also affect selective competition, it seems that some insurers are still using the incentives of NCD schemes to manipulate the balance of their portfolios between low and high risk drivers. This may suggest a certain market instability with selection against insurers with more conservative NCD schemes. If so, further retaliatory action may continue the trend towards more efficient NCD schemes and correspondingly stronger incentives for safer driving.

Although the development of the motor insurance market has produced a generation of more efficient bonus schemes than those of a decade ago, even the present day schemes are relatively inefficient. Only one of the schemes examined can provide an efficiency coefficient which, at its peak, exceeds 0·5 and even this is very much less efficient over the majority of its range. It appears from information provided by insurers that the average insured produces a claim about once every three years: for this mean value of claim frequency the majority of the schemes examined rate an efficiency coefficient in the region of 0·35 to 0·38.

The motor insurance rating schemes in use in the United Kingdom have several features in common with those in use in the United States. There is

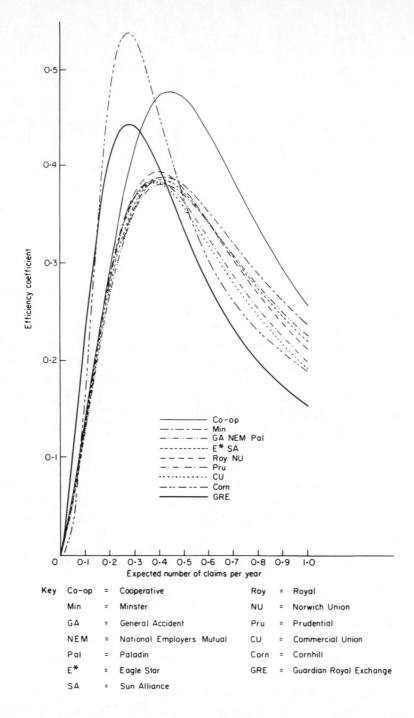

Key Co-op = Cooperative     Roy = Royal

Min = Minster     NU = Norwich Union

GA = General Accident     Pru = Prudential

NEM = National Employers Mutual     CU = Commercial Union

Pal = Paladin     Corn = Cornhill

E* = Eagle Star     GRE = Guardian Royal Exchange

SA = Sun Alliance

Fig. 6.3    Efficiency coefficients of NCD schemes in operation in 1974

100

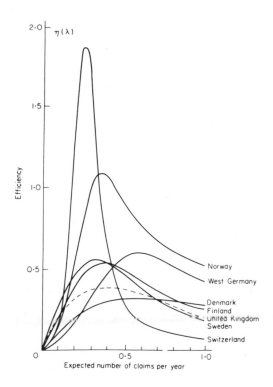

Fig. 6.4   Efficiency of NCD systems in selected European countries

also one substantial point of difference. As in the UK, American practice is normally to use a class rating structure with the main subdivisions relating to location and usage. Further subdivisions may be made for expected mileage, age, sex, marital status and vehicle characteristics. However, the use of experience rating differs. Although '... It is also common to develop individual rate modifications for insureds on the basis of their accident records'[37] experience rating has neither been used as intensively nor as extensively in the United Kingdom. Although many rating schemes do make use of loss experience in calculating the rate, many others do not. Furthermore, when experience rating is used it is often of a much cruder form than British structures. 'For example, being responsible for one accident within the past two years might increase the price of insurance by up to 30 per cent, while two accidents could cause up to a 60 per cent increase.'[38]

In contrast, Western European practice has been similar to that in Britain in that experience rating has been a fundamental part of motor insurance rating structures. Furthermore, the systems in use in many countries are more refined and more efficient than those in the UK. A comparison is drawn in Fig. 6.4 between the typical scheme currently in operation in the United Kingdom and selected schemes in operation in other Western European countries. The comparative material has been prepared by S. Vepsalainen[39] using the same measure to record the efficiency of NCD systems. It can be seen that most of the European schemes examined are more efficient over most of the relevant range than the UK scheme. Curiously, some of the European systems, particularly that of Switzerland, are overefficient over a certain range. In this case, differences between insureds in terms of expected claims cost are reflected by even larger differences in their respective net premiums.

## Premium incentives and driver response

The evolution of the British motor insurance market has led to a new generation of premium rating systems which is more solidly based on empirical data than those of a decade ago and which consequently convey increasingly efficient incentives for loss prevention. Whether insureds respond to these incentives is another matter and the difficulties of detecting such a response are immense. It might be thought that if motor insurers in unison increased their NCD scales, then the conditions for testing might prevail. In fact, this situation did occur in 1966 and there was a noticeable downturn in the number of recorded accidents. However, the timing of events proved unfortunate since the rating revisions were followed very quickly by the government's introduction of breathalyser testing for drunken driving and any change in national accident statistics may be attributable to this factor.[40] It is pertinent that much of the drop in accident frequencies was concentrated in the period 10.00$pm$ to 4.00$am$ when drunken driving is most likely to occur. This is shown in Fig. 6.5. The effects of premium incentives on accidents are swamped by a variety of other factors and the problem is one of detecting the ripples from a pebble dropped in a stormy sea.

Another possible method of testing is to compare the respective accident frequencies of two different groups of insureds, one of which is underwritten in a scheme subject to NCD and the other is in a scheme without experience rating. A few insurers operate these contrasting rating systems side by side and approaches were made to several companies to undertake an appropriate study. Of these insurers, one asserted that differences in the claims experience between the different schemes could be adequately explained by differences in the age, vehicle, location etc.,

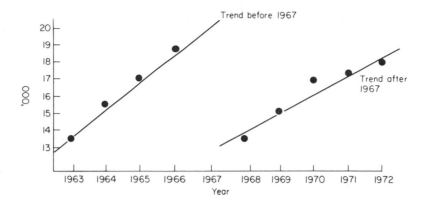

Fig. 6.5  Trends in the number of car involvements in fatal and serious accidents, 1963–72

and the composition of the portfolios and that NCD was not an important factor in explaining different accident records. The other insurers, whilst echoing the belief that NCD has an insignificant effect on accident frequencies, were unable to test this relationship, either because their records were not in a suitable form or because the samples were small and subject to large random error. The value placed upon privity of loss data was such that none of the insurers was willing to release data for appropriate testing.

The opinion that NCD may influence willingness to lodge a claim but does not significantly affect driving behaviour was unanimous amongst underwriters interviewed for this project. Whilst it would be strange indeed if the financial incentives of insurance premiums did not exert some marginal influence on driving habits, it is improbable that they form a major determinant of driver behaviour. If our concern is to use insurance premiums to manipulate the standard of driving behaviour then we are undoubtedly choosing a very inefficient instrument. However, if our concern is to achieve an efficient allocation of resources into road usage, then it is important that all costs and benefits of motoring are considered. In this context the questions of whether insurance premiums adequately reflect differences in accident cost and whether insurance contracts convey this information in a form which will provide a guide to decisionmaking are important. It is clear that competitive pressures have led to a present generation of rating structures which are undoubtedly efficient in allocating differences in expected claims costs as measured between different risk groups. However, these risk groups have largely been identified on the basis of factors which reflect the fixed costs of vehicle ownership and,

103

consequently, there are few aspects of the premium structure which bring the marginal costs of additional or less careful driving to bear on the insured. Whilst NCD schemes can potentially fill this role, it is significant that not only have they been relatively inefficient in reflecting residual differences in expected claims costs, but they also fail to convey any solid information to aid decisionmaking. The particular variable which does reflect accident costs at the margin, namely mileage, has not been exploited.

## Notes

[1] *Road Accidents in Great Britain 1973*, Department of the Environment, Scottish Development Office, Welsh Office, HMSO 1974.

[2] It is significant that the attention of non-life actuaries is directed mainly towards motor insurance.

[3] R.L. Carter, 'Competition in the British Fire and Accident Insurance Market', unpublished PhD thesis, University of Sussex, 1968, p.77.

[4] In the fire market the tariff bloc had maintained its market share because of the capacity problem and the 65/35 rule. The motor market did not have such capacity problems.

[5] See R.L. Carter, op.cit., Table 12 and discussion pp.45–64.

[6] The Consumer Association, *Which?*, January 1966.

[7] R.L. Carter, op.cit., pp.94–7.

[8] Ibid.

[9] See P.J. Franklin, 'The Reduction in the Number of Firms in the UK Motor Insurance Industry', unpublished thesis, University of Sussex, 1973, pp.13–14.

[10] Quoted from P.J. Franklin, op.cit., p.16.

[11] G. Clayton, *British Insurance*, Elek Books, London 1971, p.276.

[12] The Consumer Association, *Money Which?*, December 1969, 'Car insurance', Table 2.

[13] *Money Which?*, September 1972.

[14] See R.L. Carter, op.cit., p.72.

[15] The collapse of the Vehicle and General was attributed largely to the fact that its reserves for future claims were actuarially inadequate and that it had been relying on the expansion of premium income from an increasing share of the market. See the 'Report to the tribunal appointed to enquire into certain issues in relation to the circumstances leading up to the cessation of trading of the Vehicle and General Insurance Co. Ltd', HMSO 1972 (HL 80; HC 133), p.29.

[16] Calculations made by the Automobile Association reveal that insurance costs are in the region of 8–9 per cent of the total running costs, excluding depreciation, for a motor car. If depreciation is also taken into account, insurance will only account for about 5 per cent of total costs. However, the variation in insurance costs between motorists is very large. By way of illustration, a change in car ownership can increase premiums by up to 300 per cent; similarly, loss of NCD can cause the individual insured's premium to increase by 250 per cent. These factors suggest that changes in insurance rating factors do have some significance at the margin on total running costs. (The Automobile Association, *Drive*, Autumn 1974, p.144.)

[17] Although the use of age as the main rating factor was an important factor in the collapse of the MN & S, it cannot be concluded that its general use in rating was inappropriate. The important point was that age had been used to the exclusion of other factors. It is interesting to speculate what would have happened if the AOA had adopted the McKinsey recommendation on age related premiums. If the tariff was a genuine price leader and age had been the sole rating factor, then it may well have been commercially viable: the price leadership situation would preclude selective competition. The crucial point for the MN & S was that it stood alone.

[18] See P.J. Hall, 'The Motor Risk Statistics Bureau', *Journal of the Chartered Insurance Institute*, vol.70, 1973.

[19] The Royal's 'economy' policy.

[20] W. Vickery, 'Automobile accident, tort law, externalities and insurance: an economist's critique', *Law and Contemporary Problems*, 33, 1968, p.470.

[21] Ibid., pp.473–4.

[22] G. Clayton, op.cit., pp.276–7.

[23] See P.J. Hall, op.cit.

[24] *Road Accidents in Great Britain, 1972*, op.cit.

[25] This method may contain a significant margin of error since a sizeable proportion of the claims are estimates for outstanding claims. However, it does have the virtue of comparing like with like since it relates premiums earned and claims incurred within a given period.

[26] This system is identified as typical by H.H. Scurfield, 'Motor insurance statistics', *Journal of the Institute of Actuaries Students Society*, vol.18, part 3, August 1968.

[27] See *Money Which?*, September 1972.

[28] W. Vickery, op.cit., p.476.

[29] But slower driving can have a significant effect on the frequency of accidents. See D. Ghosh, D.S. Lees and W. Seal, 'Optimal Motorway

Speed and some Valuations of Time and Life', *Manchester School*, June 1975.

[30] K. Loimaranta, 'Some asymptotic properties of bonus systems', *Astin Bulletin*, 1970.

[31] P.D. Johnson and G.B. Hey, 'Statistical studies in motor insurance', *Journal of the Institute of Actuaries*, vol.97, part 2, no.407, December 1971, p.209.

[32] K. Loimaranta, op.cit.

[33] This is the normal elasticity formula used by economists.

[34] K. Loimaranta, op.cit.

[35] I am grateful to Mr Martin Atkins for invaluable help.

[36] Though it still did not rival the Vehicle and General scheme. There are clear reasons, however, for treating the V & G as a special case.

[37] D.L. Bicklehaupt, *General Insurance*, 9th ed., R.D. Irwin, Homewood 1974, p.155.

[38] Ibid., p.156.

[39] S. Vepsalainen, 'Applications to a theory of bonus systems', *Astin Bulletin*, 1971.

[40] See *Road Accidents in Great Britain, 1972*, op.cit., pp.x–xi.

# 7    The costs and benefits of loss prevention

The main difference in the effects of premium incentives in the fire and accident insurance markets is that, in the former, the inducements to accident prevention are very specific and usually relate to physical changes in the risk but, in the latter, incentives are largely general and behavioural. Thus a fire rating schedule contains many alternatives for the insured to adjust his premium by changing the risk. The information in the schedule is usually quite specific, though often arbitrary, and, as it becomes known, it will tend to evoke decisions on loss prevention. With motor insurance, very little hard information on risk reducing alternatives is conveyed to the insured. Although the systems distinguish between observable features such as type of car, age, occupation and location, the majority of these factors may be considered as fixed when making decisions on loss prevention. Thus it has been suggested that very few people can be expected to change jobs or move home simply to reduce their motor insurance premiums. The remaining rating feature, the no claims discount, relates to behavioural features which could radically affect loss expectancy, but fails to convey any information on specific actions which the insured might take to reduce loss expectancy and therefore his premium.

In view of the differences in information conveyed to the insured, it might be expected that incentives in fire premiums are much more effective in promoting loss prevention than motor premium incentives. There is another difference which should also be considered. In making decisions on fire protection, it is likely that the costs and benefits flowing from alternative types and levels of protection are dominated by the premium effects. After all, if the individual is fully insured, he apparently has no financial stake in losses other than those relating to his insurance premium. On the other hand, it may appear that the implications of the choice of car and different driving patterns flow far beyond the changes in insurance premium and it may be expected that these external factors will dominate the decision. This chapter discusses some of the more important effects which operate as constraints on the earlier model.

## Fiscal effects

Analysis is easy in a simple world where individuals are fully insured and where loss prevention takes the form of purchase of a safety device which has a known cost. Decisions will, rationally, involve a comparison of costs (price and cost of maintenance of the device) and benefits (current and future reductions in premiums). The decision is complicated by the fact that costs and benefits may be accruing at different points in time but there are standard techniques for coping with this problem; using discounted cash flow methods, the individual adopts that alternative which offers the highest net present value or internal rate of return. The main source of concern in this simple world is information – do premium differentials reflect differences in underwriting costs? – do they convey information on specific courses of action? – are the premium incentives known to the insured?

The real world turns out to be more complex. The schedule of costs and benefits is larger, including not only other direct financial effects but other indirect and more subtle effects. In particular, the specification of costs and benefits is affected by the structure of taxation. Where the insured is involved in business activity and liable for corporation tax, the effective costs of both insurance and loss prevention are reduced. It is fairly common practice to allow insurance premiums as a tax deductible expense and the cost of loss prevention devices may also be deductible as capital expenditure where appropriate. For example, United Kingdom taxation laws treat many items such as sprinklers and alarm systems as capital expenditure and they can consequently be written off very quickly. The formal model for identifying optimal expenditures on loss prevention developed in chapter 2 can still be preserved simply by specifying costs and benefits net of tax.

Under restrictive assumptions it can be shown that corporation tax will not disturb the insurance/loss prevention relationship. If the individual is fully insured, if he can write off all capital expenditure on loss prevention immediately for tax purposes, and if insurance premiums are tax deductible, then his welfare function can be specified as follows:

$$U = U[A - (1 - t)P(r) - (1 - t)r]$$

where $A$ is the initial wealth, $t$ is the rate of corporation tax, $P$ is the premium, and $r$ is the level of expenditure on loss prevention.

The maximising condition, using standard calculus techniques, is the level of $r$ defined as follows:

$$\frac{dU}{dr} = -U'(1-t)\left[P'(r)+1\right] = 0$$

which, assuming that the marginal utility of income $U'$ is non-zero and that the rate of taxation is not 100 per cent, implies that $P'(r) = -1$. This is the same condition which would be obtained by substituting a zero rate of tax into the welfare function and maximising in a similar fashion.

If the assumption concerning the write-off of capital expenditure is less generous, then the likely effect of taxation is that loss prevention expenditures would be somewhat lower than in the no tax case. This situation would occur, assuming positive rates of interest, if capital expenditures were not written off entirely within the year in which they were incurred but rather over a period of several years. Thus if loss prevention expenditure $r$ is written off in equal instalments over a period of $s$ years for tax purposes, then the optimal programme is defined by the condition:[1]

$$P'(r) = -\sum_{i=1}^{s} \frac{1}{s} \frac{1}{(1+d)^i}$$

where $d$ is the rate of discount, which implies a lower level of expenditure than under the no tax case defined above by the condition $P'(r) = -1$.

Taxation might also affect expenditures on loss prevention by influencing the chosen level of insurance protection. Again there are offsetting effects. On the one hand, insurance premiums are usually tax deductible but so too are uninsured losses. However, with respect to losses, they may be sufficiently large to wipe out profits and practice varies between countries as to the extent to which trading losses may be carried over to subsequent years. The general effect, as measured by two studies which appraise corporate performance in terms of the rate of growth of assets,[2] is that high levels of taxation tend to favour low levels of insurance. Thus whilst high levels of taxation might, in given circumstances, lead to a misallocation of loss prevention resources, there is an offsetting effect since in reducing the level of insurance protection they will tend to minimise the distortions introduced by non-discriminatory insurance premiums.

Finally, corporation tax only applies to insurance premiums and expenditures on loss prevention insofar as they affect trading profits. A further prospect is that fiscal controls could be selectively used in order to counter the allocative distortions which result from inefficient premium structures. The possible use of such premium taxes is discussed in the next chapter.

## Residual monetary losses

Amongst the various costs and benefits of loss prevention, there is one particular set of benefits which reflect the limitations of the analysis of this study. As a simplifying assumption, the model of chapter 2 related to the principle of indemnity. When an individual is fully insured and his policy is one of indemnity, he will be fully compensated for losses; he thus has no direct financial stake in those losses. In a financial sense he may be said to be indifferent as to whether losses occur or not. Where losses can be completely and unambiguously measured in money terms, the benefits of insurance can be fully exploited. However, there are other types of loss where monetary valuation is not practicable because the loss has far reaching consequences which interact with other extraneous factors. Events such as fire, explosion, injury to employees, machine breakdown etc. interrupt the process of production and sales. The firm will be unable to maintain its revenue and yet it will still have a continuing commitment to meet fixed costs. Consequently, profits will decline.

Interruption losses depend on the ease and rapidity with which destroyed or damaged articles can be replaced. In turn, this will depend on the degree of sophistication and specialisation embodied in the technology and on market conditions facing the suppliers of those goods. With a specialised technology, and where supplying firms are operating at full capacity, the interruption loss will be severe. The opposite conditions make for small interruption loss. A second factor determining the severity of business interruption is the degree of interdependence between separate processes within the firm. Clearly, the interruption loss is likely to be most severe where the web of interconnections is thickest. A third factor is the state of competition and demand in the market in which the firm produces. Conditions of high level of demand, low consumer loyalty, absence of buffer stocks, competitors operating with surplus capacity, and absence of collusion between firms will lead to severe interruption loss.

The event which causes material loss also sparks off the interruption loss. Therefore forms of loss prevention which reduce the probability of material loss also reduce the probability of interruption loss. But other forms of loss prevention may be aimed directly at interruption loss and have little or no effect on material loss. Examples are: maintenance of buffer stocks, subdivision and separation of production and other operational units, diversification of outlets and sources of supply, and the negotiation of reciprocal production agreements with competitors.

Clearly, the firm will derive private benefit from these forms of loss prevention. Their success will minimise the loss of production, loss of market share and therefore loss of short and long term profits. The social utility of these forms of loss prevention is less clear. The loss of production for one firm does not necessarily imply loss of production for the economy as a whole; it may or may not be made good by others. For example, if other firms in the industry operate at full capacity, then either industry production will fall or it will only be maintained by diverting resources from elsewhere. There will be both a private loss and a social loss. On the other hand, if competing firms can make good the lost production by using idle resources, then the loss will be solely internal to the firm. In practice, a situation in which firms can step up production without any increase in costs can rarely, if ever, be found. But there are cases where factors are not fully utilised and it may be generally true that the social loss, though not zero, is something less than the private loss to the firm.

The discussion is further complicated by vertical interdependence between firms. A fire in one firm could (a) deprive its own customers of a source of supply and interrupt their business, and (b) deprive its own sources of supply of an outlet for their products and so interrupt their business. Therefore whilst a fire or similar event may bring windfall gains to competitors, it may also impose sudden losses on trading partners.

As business interruption is usually insurable[3] across a similar range of hazards as material damage insurance it may also be expected to have consequences for loss prevention similar to those of the latter; the process of risk transfer undermines incentives for loss prevention and these incentives may, or may not, be replaced by premium incentives. Since the normal formula is to provide compensation for the loss of gross profit attributable to the insured event and a contribution towards the fixed costs which have to be met from diminished profits, the indirect financial sanction of loss is removed.

It is standard practice to base rates of premium for business interruption insurance on the rates for material damage insurance and consequently any inducement for loss prevention under material damage insurance is reinforced through the interruption insurance premium. The *quid pro quo* is that any distortions or omissions in the material damage premium are transferred to the business interruption premium. Further manipulation is then made to account for factors which are peculiar to the interruption risk, such as the degree of interdependence, diversification, contingency planning, market conditions etc. These adjustments are often based on a special business interruption survey but since the relevant features are difficult to measure, even though they may be easily observed, they are not amenable to statistical analysis. Adjustments therefore tend to be subjective rather than empirical.

There are other important differences between the loss prevention effects of material damage and business interruption insurance. Since the social value of expenditures to reduce interruption loss is less clear than that for direct loss, the premium incentives must also be interpreted differently. At one extreme, it can be argued that if lost production can be made good by employing idle resources, then expenditure to reduce business loss is socially wasteful. It neither increases nor minimises the reduction in wealth but simply alters the distribution of profits and incomes within the industry. Following this argument through, the optimal insurance arrangement is one which *destroys* incentives for loss prevention. However, this solution not only relies on a particular set of market conditions but also incorporates a particular set of value judgements concerning the distribution of income. An alternative rough and ready rule which, on balance, may be preferable is that social welfare might be best served if premium differentials simply reflected differences in underwriting costs. This rule (a) assumes that the loss of production to the firm is also a loss to the society, (b) contains an implicit value judgement in favour of the *status quo* and (c) neatly coincides with the model of optimal insurer behaviour.

The second important difference lies in the inability of business interruption insurance to insulate the firm from the full implications of major losses. Whilst insurance may make good lost profits and meet fixed costs for one, two or even five years, it cannot do so in perpetuity. But the consequences of the event may be permanent. If a firm is out of business for some considerable time, it may suffer permanent loss of customers, suffer a permanent decline of its share of the market and will forego any speculative opportunities that occur during the period over which it is out of operation. The weight of these losses can be very heavy indeed. For example, one study of American firms showed that 43 per cent of companies suffering serious fires disappeared from the market immediately afterwards, despite insurance coverage, and a further 28 per cent did not survive for more than three years.[4] Of course, there may be several reasons for this. The statistics may include cases of arson and others where the firm's performance was poor and, although the fire was accidental, it simply provided the opportunity for discussing exit from the market. For other firms which might well have been achieving satisfactory performance, protracted absence from the market following a serious loss permits customers and competing firms to establish new trading patterns. It then becomes difficult, if not impossible, for the firm to re-establish its former position.

Business interruption insurance is therefore not subject to the principle of indemnity. It provides a temporary offset against lost profit which may well provide adequate protection for the small to medium size losses but can never provide full protection from larger and more spectacular losses. No matter how much business interruption insurance is purchased, the insured retains a stake in the interruption losses. He will therefore benefit directly from loss prevention, quite apart from any reductions in insurance premiums, and thus risk transfer will be unable to eliminate loss prevention incentives. The potency of this residual incentive was revealed in the responses of the AIRMIC members discussed in chapter 5 from which it appeared that business interruption rivalled premium reductions as a stimulus for evoking loss prevention decisions.

## Non-monetary effects

Losses which are normally measured in subjective terms and which are personal to the insured are often called psychic losses. The particular feature of these losses is that, whilst in principle they may be subject to the measuring rod of money, they are not usually valued by the economic process.[5] For example, life and limb have no marketable value (though in an age of transplant surgery this may no longer be strictly true), yet to the owner and his relations their value may be very high or even infinite.

The weight of these problems is such that insurance typically does not cover sentimental or psychic loss, though there are important exceptions. In the first place, insurers will sometimes adopt a more flexible attitude to claims settlement when psychic loss is present and, secondly, agreed value policies are sometimes available in which the amount to be paid is fixed at the inception of the policy. The insured is then able to fix the sum insured at a level which reflects his personal valuation of the loss. In general, however, the insurance settlement is based on objective indicators.

The general exclusion of psychic loss from insurance coverage defines limits on the extent to which insurance incentives can influence expenditures on loss prevention. Formally, the effect is to introduce an element of self-insurance so that, even with non-discriminatory premiums, there are still residual incentives for the insured to protect his risk. However, since there are difficulties of objective valuation, the model now defies outside scrutiny: it is not possible to identify the optimum or to monitor whether the insured is behaving rationally.[6] Thus whilst directional changes in loss prevention expenditure can be anticipated, their magnitude cannot. Where psychic losses are important the model developed in the previous chapters loses precision.

Equally important are the non-monetary costs of loss prevention. Where loss prevention involves the purchase of a safety device the cost is easily measured. But loss prevention might alternatively involve behavioural change and then costs can only be measured in terms of opportunities foregone. For example, the practice of safer driving might involve costs in terms of time, the sacrifice of the pleasures of fast driving and the non-fulfilment of personality traits which may largely determine driver behaviour. These effects add to the uncertainties of the model as a predictive instrument.

In examining the various costs and benefits of loss prevention, the subject matter of this study is put into wider perspective. The relationship between insurance pricing and loss prevention may, or may not, be a sensitive one. For those activities where there is already an established financial basis for decisionmaking and where insurance premiums form an important item in the schedule of costs and benefits of loss prevention, the response to premium incentives will tend to be sharp. These conditions are likely to prevail in the case of industrial fire insurance. For other activities, highlighted by private motoring, the role of insurance incentives, whilst it may not be peripheral, is not dominating. Financial incentives as a whole may only play a supporting role in determining driving behaviour, the main determinants being of a non-financial nature.

## Notes

[1] This is obtained by using the welfare function:

$$U = U \left[ A - (1-t)\,P(r) - (1-t) \sum_{i=1}^{s} \frac{r}{s} \frac{1}{(1+d)^i} \right]$$

and differentiating with respect to $r$ to get:

$$\frac{dU}{dr} = U'\,(1-t) \left[ P'(r) - \sum_{i=1}^{s} \frac{1}{s} \frac{1}{(1+d)^i} \right] = 0$$

The condition in the text again assumes $U' \neq 0$ and $t \neq 1$.

[2] See A.E. Hofflander, E. Renshaw and V. Renshaw, 'Optimal insurance', *Journal of Risk and Insurance*, vol.38, no.2, June 1971, and M.H. Atkins, N.A. Doherty and R.L. Carter, 'Risk, insurance and the growing firm', University of Nottingham Discussion Papers in Industrial Economics No.2.

[3] It is alternatively known as business interruption insurance, loss of profits insurance and consequential loss insurance. Its main application is in the field of fire and associated perils and machine breakdown. Material damage insurance is normally a precondition to insurance of the interruption risk.

[4] Centre National de Prevention et Protection, *Face au Risque.*

[5] For a recent example of the prospects of such valuations see M.H. Cooper and A.J. Culyer, 'The price of blood: an economic study of the charitable and commercial principle,' *Hobart Paper No.41,* Institute of Economic Affairs, London.

[6] Although a subjective element is already present in the parameters of the individual's utility function.

# 8   Some policy implications

The implications of insurance for social welfare may be developed along the following lines. The mechanics of risk spreading are such that as an increasing number of risks are pooled the relative variance of each risk diminishes.[1] Since the quality of variability in the level of future income or wealth is widely assumed to have a disutility value, risk spreading can simultaneously increase the welfare of each participant.[2] This is subject to the proviso that the transaction costs borne by each individual do not overwhelm the gain in terms of increased security in future income. Furthermore, these welfare gains must also be offset against, or aggregated to, a further set of welfare effects which arise from the interdependence between insurance and loss prevention activities.

The effects which insurance has on loss prevention activities can be described by three interrelated mechanisms. First, risk transfer destroys incentives which may otherwise encourage the insured to avoid losses; secondly, insurance premiums may create a system of secondary incentives for loss prevention; thirdly, premium incentives also act as a channel for information on different forms of loss prevention. The 'worst' and 'best' permutations of these functions can be represented as follows. On the one hand, there is the extreme moral hazard argument that insurance will generate indifference and carelessness since it removes financial incentives to avoid loss. This effect can potentially negate the welfare case for insurance protection.[3] Conversely, the insurance function may be seen as one in which reliable information on different forms of loss prevention is disseminated in premium structures and is reinforced by appropriate premium incentives; therefore insurance does not relax incentives for loss prevention but simply improves the information upon which decisions are made. Not surprisingly, the conclusions which have been reached here are to be found between these two extreme views.

It has been suggested that '. . . encouragement of loss prevention in rate making is not difficult to achieve but is often lost along the way'.[4] This failure of insurers to achieve premium structures which efficiently discriminate between different risks and contain appropriate incentives for loss prevention may be largely attributable to the restraints on effective price competition between insurers. The widespread tendency to form cartels suggests that each individual insurer is willing to forego the profit

116

advantages which may accrue from a finer subdivision of its portfolio into appropriate risk groupings in favour of the increased stability resulting from cartel control of the market. The cartels have been widely criticised for their failure to innovate and to improve the statistical basis for their rates despite the potential advantages of pooled data. Governments, for their part, have adopted a somewhat permissive attitude towards insurer cartels and have not usually interfered with the collection and use of empirical data. The main challenge to the cartels and the main stimulus to discriminatory rating has come from the deviant insurers who have, at least in some markets, competed vigorously for selected risks.

The policy issues which are discussed below relate to the social welfare and to the narrower interests of both insurers and insureds.

## Social policy

Considerations of social welfare open discussion concerning the question of government intervention in insurance activity. Within the context of a private economy, the role of government may be seen as removing those obstacles which prevent market forces from achieving an efficient allocation of resources. At least three such constraints are commonly discussed by economists: externalities, monopoly power and the spread of information.

Externalities are said to exist when the activities of one person impose costs and benefits upon others. With such a wide definition of externality, the contract of insurance may be said to create an external cost: the financial cost of some hazard is 'externalised' from the insured to the insurer; consequently, the insured fails to consider this cost in decisions on loss prevention; thus resources are misallocated. One remedy in such cases is for the government to impose a corrective tax.[5] If insurers fail to provide premium incentives for loss prevention, the government can alternatively provide fiscal incentives. However, it has been argued that where there is adequate information, the problem can be resolved by bargaining between the parties.[6] The argument has added force where the parties are bound together in a contractual relationship, since the conditions surrounding the contract bring the parties together in a bargaining situation and the terms of the contract, notably the premium, can be manipulated to mutual advantage.[7] The theoretical analysis of this study suggests that in a well-oiled competitive insurance market the total effect of private bargains would be to render such corrective fiscal incentives redundant. However, the empirical findings, whilst confirming the effects of competitive mechanisms, also identify market and informational constraints which cause the market process to fall short of an optimal solution.

In considering the case for a tax or subsidy it is helpful to differentiate between failure to achieve an efficient allocation of expenses between insureds and failure to achieve an efficient allocation of claims costs. In the first case, the most likely form of failure is that expenses are charged to insureds as a proportionate loading on the expected claim cost whereas the true imposition of costs is of the composite form described in chapter 2. The optimum incentives are thus of the form:

$$P = a_1 C + a_2$$

where $P$ is the premium payable, $C$ is the expected claim cost and $a_1$ and $a_2$ are parameters. The actual incentives are of the form:

$$P = a_3 C$$

The corrective tax can therefore be specified as:

$$T = (a_1 - a_3)C + a_2$$

which could well turn out to be negative, i.e. a subsidy. The collection, or at least the calculation, of the tax may well be left to insurers. But if this were the case, it could be argued that if the insurer can calculate the tax he can also calculate the optimal premium structure and he would have a profit incentive to use such premiums. Thus the case for a corrective tax may fall apart.

The case for a corrective tax to offset distortions in the allocation of claims costs seems equally unimpressive. The need for such a tax arises from information failures, yet these same information constraints may undermine the ability to calculate the level of the tax. If insurers are to calculate the tax it is difficult to explain why they have not already used the necessary information in devising premiums. If the task were left to a government department they would still have to rely on claims information supplied by insurers. A more useful direction to government intervention lies with the removal of those constraints which prevent insurers themselves from devising efficient premium structures.

Anti-monopoly activity has a long history in Western Europe and North America, though its application to insurance has been somewhat restrained due largely to the fear that unbridled competition would bring widespread bankruptcies. Cartels have been permitted to exist and, in many cases, encouraged, though their use of monopoly power has been subjected to government restraint. The present analysis suggests that the dissolution of the cartels will lead to more efficient discrimination in rating

118

structures although it is unclear whether this would also be accompanied by a spasm of company failures. Certainly, the UK motor market has settled down and, it is argued here, improved rating structures; furthermore, it is argued by the Monopolies Commission that the break-up of the fire tariff would not lead to destructive competition. In any case, control of solvency requirements provides an alternative 'fine tuner' mechanism which can be directed solely at insurer solvency.

Perhaps the most fertile area for government intervention is the stimulation of the collection and flow of statistical information. Statistics can be assembled either privately or collectively. Where rating is by cartel, the pooling of statistics emerges as a by-product of the rating function. Consequently, the advantages of large sample size are reaped for the benefit of both insurers and insureds alike; collective data provide a more reliable guide to loss expectancies. However, the offsetting costs lie in the rigidities of the price fixing agreement and its exclusion of rating innovations by individual members. In a competitive market, there may still be collective benefits to insurers from the pooling of statistics yet these must be offset against the competitive advantages to individual insurers from rating innovations based on private information. Thus a competitive market structure may be accompanied by the pooling of statistics (examples are life and motor insurance in the United Kingdom) or it may not (as in other branches of non-life insurance in the UK).

The proper activity of government may be to encourage insurers to cooperate more actively in the collection of statistics or even to establish the appropriate mechanisms itself. The first prospect of a pool run by insurers themselves appears the more feasible since it can use the skills already in the industry. The existence of collective statistics need not discourage innovation by individual insurers and this has certainly not been the result in the UK motor market. However, there are advantages for building in mechanisms for monitoring and, if necessary, revising the framework for collecting information. The revision mechanism could take the form of a research unit with the function of experimenting with new and improved models for correlating loss frequencies with appropriate explanatory factors and reporting to a suitable body with executive authority to revise the statistical framework. The statistical bureau would not be a rating bureau but would simply make available processed statistical information with no requirements as to how it should be used. This is similar to the role of the Motor Risk Statistics Bureau.

A second fruitful area for government activity concerns the availability of information. The dissemination of loss prevention information in the form of premium differentials is second best to the statistics upon which the premiums are based. This basic information would be invaluable to those involved in research into loss prevention and for large buyers of insurance and their brokers, yet insurers have chosen to keep this information to themselves. There are strong welfare reasons for giving such information wider currency. First, it promotes efficient decisionmaking on loss prevention. Secondly, it also promotes efficient decisions on the amount of insurance to purchase so that any distortions in loss prevention incentives in insurance premiums are not compounded by the purchase of too much or too little insurance. Thirdly, it may stimulate an external feedback on the adequacy of statistics and their use in rating systems. Fourthly, it may be valuable to researchers and manufacturers who wish to measure the effectiveness of safety devices or the hazards associated with construction materials, industrial processes etc.

One area in which these various issues assume a topical interest is the current debate which is taking place both here and in other countries about the reform of civil liability for actions which cause death or personal injury. The main relevant component of the legal system is the law of negligence which is more popularly known as the fault system. This system redistributes the monetary costs of certain accidents in which it can be shown that, according to legal definition, one party has been 'at fault'. The objectives of the fault system are rarely made explicit and when they are there is rarely a consensus as to what they may be. The most common contentions are that the system is a compensation system or that it is a system of deterrence which regulates the incidence of accidents by the financial penalties which are imposed by the courts. If the second objective is imputed to the fault system then it might be claimed that fulfilment is frustrated by the prevalence of insurance against third party liability; the deterrent effect is removed since it is the insurance company which pays the damages. This argument is only impressive if the rating system fails to transmit these incentives in the form of premium differentials. In fact, the counter-argument can be taken a stage further along the lines that if insurance rating is effective in terms of risk discrimination, then it is a far more efficient way of regulating accidents since it disseminates information on those forms of behaviour which will reduce loss expectancy. Without insurance the threat of a possible court action from a possible future accident remains a remote event which the individual will find difficult to relate to current behaviour. The policy recommendation might very well be that if financial regulation of certain accident producing activities is required, then insurance, if it is properly rated, is a useful policy instrument.

The role of government in a mixed economy includes the ownership and control of production activities. The issues raised by public ownership take us far beyond the present study. Therefore the only pertinent comment to be made in the present context is that government insurance activities have tended to sacrifice discriminatory rating, and its consequences for loss prevention, in favour of wider social objectives. The consequent loss of economic efficiency is not a necessary outcome of public ownership but, if it does arise, it may not be an insignificant cost and should therefore be thrown into the overall balance of costs and benefits.

## Insurers

There was a time when it was thought that enlightened self-interest would promote social well-being. It is suggested here that the promotion of discriminatory rating would benefit insurers and also encourage an efficient allocation of resources into loss prevention activities. Government action may be redundant since rating innovations would increase profitability both for the innovating insurer and for the industry as a whole. However, the industry has been slow to innovate and rating structures have tended to fossilise. The reasons are complex and include the historical paucity of statistical/actuarial skills in non-life insurance, the threat to market stability from rating innovations and the apparent willingness to accept satisfactory, rather than maximum, levels of profit. Consequently, premium structures have been largely based on subjective judgement with only broad adjustment to actual loss experience. The empirical adjustment has normally involved varying the overall level of rates for a broad class of risks with little attempt to establish accurate differentials in the premiums paid by individual risks within the class.

The 'rule of thumb' approach to rating, whilst it may have produced satisfactory levels of profit in times of economic stability, has been found to be lacking in times of rapid economic change, often with fatal consequences for insurers. Insurers are becoming increasingly aware of the advantages of establishing a sounder empirical base to their rating and there is growing activity in the collection and collation of non-life statistics. This is most readily noticed in the emergence of what to the UK market is an entirely new breed – the non-life actuary.

The policy issues for insurers go far beyond exploiting a happy coincidence between private and social interest. They also call for a recognition and discharge of so-called 'social responsibilities'. The relationships which a firm has with the public, with its employees and with the government can often be improved if its activities take account not only of the welfare of its managers and shareholders but also of employees and other groups outside the corporate net. The field of loss prevention in particular is one in which the social performance of insurers will almost certainly influence government policy. Thus at the time of writing the Committee of Enquiry under Lord Pearson[8] is sitting to consider civil liability for accidents and the range of possible outcomes must certainly include some in which insurance functions are transferred to the State, as, for example, under the Woodhouse scheme in New Zealand.[9] The allocative issues considered in this book are certainly pertinent to this discussion.

The call for recognition of social responsibility has been heard most recently in the field of pollution where many firms anticipate government action or set themselves higher standards in the discharge of noxious wastes than those required by law. For their part, insurers are shouldering wider responsibilities in relation to losses than the simple transfer of risk. This is evident in the promotion of research, the establishment of agencies for the dissemination of technical advice on loss prevention and from the stress on loss prevention in insurers' advertising campaigns. Two other areas which may be prescribed for the discharge of social responsibility, and which pre-empt the case for government activity, are the formation of collective statistics and the widespread dissemination of this statistical material.

As stated above, collusion in the formation of statistics, without collusion in rating, may result spontaneously in competitive market conditions. Where it does not, it might be supposed that either the appropriate institutions to assemble insurers for discussion do not exist, or that there is no will to co-operate because insurers value private gain higher than the gain to insurers as a whole. Certainly, the appropriate forum exists in the British Insurance Association in the United Kingdom (and similar bodies elsewhere) and its committees would do well to consider the balance between these private gains and the social gains accruing outside the insurance sector from collective data.

Whilst there may be a clear private gain for an insurer from not releasing his statistics unilaterally to competitors, the case for keeping collective statistics out of the hands of consumers, brokers, government agencies and research organisations is not so clear. There are fears that the material is too complex and, since it is assembled for a specific purpose, may be misunderstood. Also it is feared that the widespread availability of loss data might promote self-insurance in the form of captive insurance companies and large deductibles. On the other hand, distinct social benefits from a freer flow of information have been identified. Again, insurers may do well to balance the private and social benefits from the circulation of their data and they might also weigh in the balance the mistrust and suspicion that secrecy brings. In an age of collective bargaining by labour and consumers and of intensive government regulation of the private sector of the economy, the discharge of social responsibility by firms may simply involve a trade-off between short term profitability and long term profitability or even survival.

Other areas for corrective action by insurers include the limitation of insurance protection by use of deductibles and other risk sharing devices to reduce moral hazard and in devising alternative forms of loss finance which avoid moral hazard altogether. The use of risk sharing devices can be considered on two levels. First, insurers might withhold full insurance protection to combat moral hazard or, second, insurers might make available to the insured a wider choice in the depth of protection. The first of these devices can only be considered as a second best solution since, in reducing moral hazard, it sacrifices the benefits of risk transfer outlined at the beginning of this chapter; premium discrimination does not involve this trade-off. On the other hand, the insured may wish to choose a high level of deductible in order to avoid much of the insurance transaction cost but is prevented from doing so by the insurer – thus the FOC limits deductibles to £10,000. Certainly, the removal of these constraints on risk sharing gets rid of an unnecessary obstacle to the efficient allocation of resources.

A second device which might be considered is the use of contingency loans for financing losses. Under this system, the individual has access only to loan facilities in the event of loss. This solves the liquidity problem of financing the loss without removing the financial responsibility for payment of the loss. Its attraction is that interest payments on the loan may be much cheaper than the expense loading on the insurance policy. Thus whilst the benefits of risk transfer are foregone, there may be instances in which this form of finance is preferable.[10] The wider implications of such schemes need further research but it may be noted here that they are not accompanied by an erosion of incentives for loss prevention. There may be a *prima facie* case for making available such facilities on a limited basis to support the retained risk on a deductible etc. in a conventional insurance policy.

Finally, the relationships outlined in this study suggest a *prima facie* case for insurers to diversify into the loss prevention business. Without insurance there might be a large latent demand for loss prevention devices since individuals would then carry their own risks. If insurance is introduced, the demand becomes real, the net effect of insurance being for insurers to establish the cost effectiveness of different types of loss prevention by observing statistical patterns over their portfolios and to disseminate this information amongst insureds in the form of premium differentials. Viewed in terms of investment opportunities, the role of insurance is to prime the market for loss prevention services. Evidence of the potential benefits to the producers of loss prevention devices can be seen in the pressures they exert in trying to gain recognition of their products in the insurers' rating schedules. Certainly, with sprinklers, the admission or exclusion of a particular product from the FOC list of approved sprinklers can substantially determine its commercial future. What is surprising is that these spillovers have not been exploited on a more formal basis.

In the United States the Factory Mutual System provides both insurance and loss prevention services. Admittedly, the Factory Mutual has evolved from a different economic and institutional background to that of British insurers with more direct state intervention in the rating process. However, it is still rather difficult to understand why British insurers, having created an effective market for loss prevention equipment, have failed to step in as producers. Perhaps the first tentative moves in this direction are currently being witnessed with the deployment of insurance surveyors, and the recruitment by insurers of specialist staff, to offer loss prevention consultancy services.

Whilst it may be difficult to understand why insurers have been slow to diversify into the loss prevention business, it is not so difficult to understand why the public interest may not be best served by such a development. The problem lies with the presence of monopoly powers or inefficiency in either of these markets. Thus a monopoly insurer might concentrate on one type of loss prevention device in its rating schedule to the exclusion of other effective devices in order to reap economies of scale in the production of its loss prevention equipment. Alternatively, if the firm has monopoly powers in the market for loss prevention equipment, it might deliberately overstate the insurance premium reduction in its captive insurance operation, thereby forcing other insurers to follow suit, and thus reap excessive profits in the loss prevention equipment market. A third factor is that a dynamic and independent loss prevention industry would provide pressure for discriminatory rating on an otherwise inefficient insurance industry. The take-over of the loss prevention operations would probably remove any innovatory stimulus.

## Insureds

The effect of insurance on the optimal loss prevention programme for an insured underlines the need for a co-ordinated financial strategy for dealing with risk situations. The important policy implications lie in the use of this interdependence to reduce overall (insurance plus loss prevention) expenditure on risk situations. This suggests that there is a financial return to be made from investing in information on the available opportunities for reducing loss probabilities and in information on insurers' premium structures. Insurance market information has traditionally been supplied by insurance brokers but until recently there has been little attempt to provide a more comprehensive consultancy service which co-ordinates loss prevention advisory services with insurance market services. These composite risk management services have been substantially developed in the United States and, after the customary transatlantic lag, they are now being explored in the United Kingdom. Certainly, American experience suggests that there is growth potential for these services and this in part reflects the potential gains to insureds from co-ordinating their loss prevention programme with their insurance cover.

There are limits on the extent to which an insured can use an effective loss prevention measure to manipulate his insurance premiums. Insurance pricing policies are not perfect and do not pick up all loss prevention devices. It has been suggested that these situations are unstable from a market point of view since competition between insurers will lead to more discriminatory rating structures. However, there are also policy implications for the individual insured. The situation is also unstable from an individual bargaining viewpoint. If the formal premium structure fails to reflect the cost effectiveness of a particular loss prevention device, then informal bargaining can be of benefit to insured and insurer alike. Any premium reduction which is greater than the cost of the loss prevention device and less than the reduction in the expected value of loss (assuming the latter is the greater amount) is mutually beneficial. Whilst the possibility of effective bargaining of this nature may not be plausible for the individual or small firm it is certainly plausible for the large corporate insured or for groups of insureds acting in concert through the medium of brokers.

Bargaining for premium reduction may be most likely where the cost effectiveness of the loss prevention device can be readily demonstrated. However, it may still be possible even when the efficiency of the device cannot be properly established. Depending upon the statistical characteristics of the risk, it may be possible to infer its efficiency from subsequent loss experience and an experience adjustment can then be incorporated in the premium structure.

In the same way that a conflict can arise between the individual and collective interests of insurers, a similar conflict can arise between the individual and collective interests of insureds. If it is true that insureds as a group bear the costs and reap the benefits of loss prevention, then their collective interests will be best served if each individual selects that level of loss prevention which balances the marginal costs and benefits regardless of whether these costs and benefits are borne by him or passed on to the insurer under the insurance contract. This solution will minimise the total cost of fires, explosions, injuries and similar losses to insureds as a whole and it will be encouraged where insurers build the appropriate premium incentives into the insurance contract.

The proposition that costs and benefits of loss prevention are confined to insureds as a group cannot be taken without qualification, though it may offer a rough approximation. For example, the benefits of loss prevention may be initially reaped by the insurance company shareholders in the form of increased profits but, in the longer term, competitive pressures are likely to transform excess profits into lower premiums. Similarly, if there are interdependencies in production, then the effects of loss prevention by one individual firm may be felt by its competitors and trading partners as discussed in chapter 7. But these third parties may themselves be insured and, if so, these costs and benefits are internal to the insuring sector. Thus the case for discriminatory rating is supported by consideration of the collective interests of insureds.

Whilst there is a collective interest, it is not directly represented. Some protection is provided by consumer associations, though they have not played a major role in the insurance field. Public control has attempted to achieve discriminatory rating, particularly in the United States where a system of 'not unfairly discriminatory' ratings is an explicit policy objective. However, in the United Kingdom, the force of state intervention has been concentrated on the regulation of solvency requirements.[11] Where insureds' interests are represented by brokers a collective bargaining situation can arise but here the broker's market power is normally used for the individual benefit of his clients – to optimise the terms and conditions of insurance for each of his clients.

The conflict between collective and individual interests of insureds arises when premiums fail to discriminate between insureds. Premiums thus tend to be averaged within a rating class with low risk insureds paying more than is appropriate on actuarial grounds and high risk insureds paying something less. This system provides an effective subsidy from low

126

to high risk insureds and a move to a more efficiently discriminatory rating system would consequently shift income in favour of low risk insureds. Certainly, these income distributions need to be evaluated and the notions of unfair discrimination and equity in premium rating imply a positive social valuation on movements in this direction.

For the insured, the financially optimal policy with regard to loss prevention will take account of the presence of insurance and the conditions of protection; these factors will influence rational decisionmaking. This statement turns the moral hazard argument on its head. It has been said that insurance disseminates information on the effectiveness of different forms of loss prevention. It cannot simultaneously be argued that insureds should use these signals in the premium structure to guide their decisions *and* that the programme of loss prevention should be invariant with respect to the presence, degree or conditions of insurance protection. Apart from the limited case of fraudulent behaviour, if moral hazard does arise, it may be attributable to the failure of insurance premiums to convey the appropriate financial incentives or to inform the insured of those particular actions which will reduce his loss expectancy.

Throughout this book it has been assumed that the relationship between insurance and loss prevention has been a one-sided affair. The optimal loss prevention programme has depended upon the extent and the conditions of insurance coverage. However, the reasons for extending the causal connection in the other direction are just as impressive. Loss prevention can provide a substitute for insurance. In the extreme, loss prevention can be so effective that it reduces the probability of loss to zero, thereby removing all reason for the purchase of insurance. Short of this extreme, the extent of the substitution of loss prevention for insurance depends upon individual risk preferences, the effective price of insurance and the extent to which loss prevention reduces the variability (as opposed to the expected value) of prospective future loss. It can be shown that different forms of loss prevention can have different statistical effects on the shape of the insured's loss probability distribution, even though they might be equally effective in reducing the expected value of loss. Loss prevention can be classified according to whether it operates by reducing the size of loss (common examples are internal fire brigades, detectors and alarms) or whether it operates by removing some of the possible causes of loss without having much effect on the size of losses which do occur (examples are maintenance and servicing schedules, safety campaigns and the use of anti-theft devices). The former tend to be relatively more effective at reducing the variation in the possible size of future losses than the latter.

127

For example, if an insured can effectively subdivide his factory into separate sections by the construction of party walls so that there is very little chance of a fire spreading from one section to another, then he might well wish to limit his insurance protection to catastrophe cover.

These considerations illustrate the case for submerging the relationship between insurance and loss prevention into a wider set of risk management relationships. Risks can be transferred, retained, removed or reduced. All the techniques of modern management can be brought into play to exploit the interdependence between these strategies and to formulate a financially optimal risk management programme. This is far removed from the traditional tenets of the old corporate insurance manager who saw insurance purchasing as common prudence, quite regardless of the cost, and who looked upon loss prevention as a moral virtue yet was left quite unaware of its possible scope.

## Notes

[1] The statistical mechanism is known as the law of large numbers. For an application to insurance problems see section 2 (G. Dickinson) in Carter and Doherty (eds), *Handbook of Risk Management*, Kluwer Harrap, 1974.

[2] See K.J. Arrow, *Aspects of the Theory of Risk Bearing*, Helsinki, 1965.

[3] M.V. Pauly, 'The economics of moral hazard', *American Economic Review*, June 1968, p.58.

[4] R.I. Mehr and E. Cammack, *Principles of Insurance*, 5th ed., R.D. Irwin, Homewood p.645.

[5] For a critique of this practice see J.M. Buchannan and W.C. Stubblebine, 'Externality', *Economica*, vol.29, 1962; and H. Shibata, 'Pareto optimality, trade and the Pigovian tax', *Economica*, vol.39, 1972.

[6] See R.H. Coase, 'The problem of social cost', *Journal of Law and Economics*, vol.3, 1960.

[7] See O.E. Williamson, D.G. Olson and A. Ralston, 'Externalities, insurance and disability analysis', *Economica*, vol.35, 1967.

[8] The Royal Commission on Civil Liability and Compensation for Personal Injury, appointed March 1973.

[9] *Compensation for Personal Injury in New Zealand*, Report of the Royal Commission of Inquiry, December 1967.

[10] See M.H. Atkins, N.A. Doherty and R.L. Carter, 'Risk, insurance

and the growing firm', University of Nottingham Discussion Papers in Industrial Economics No.2, 1974.

[11] Particularly since, at the time of writing, there has been no government action on the Monopolies Commission recommendation.

# Index

# The author

Neil Doherty undertook the research for this book while he was Stewart Wrightson Research Fellow at the University of Nottingham. Previously he had lectured in Economics at the Universities of York and Zambia, and he has worked in the insurance industry in both companies and broking. Since 1975 he has been an Economic Adviser at the Department of Health and Social Security.

# Other SAXON HOUSE publications

| | |
|---|---|
| Hodges, M. | *Multinational corporations and national governments* |
| Liggins, D. | *National economic planning in France* |
| Friedly, P. H. | *National policy responses to urban growth* |
| Madelin, H. | *Oil and politics* |
| Tilford, R. (ed.) | *The Ostpolitik and political change in Germany* |
| Friedrichs, J., H. Ludtke | *Participant observation* |
| Fitzmaurice, J. | *The party groups in the European parliament* |
| Brown, J., G. Howes (eds) | *The police and the community* |
| Lang, R. W. | *The politics of drugs* |
| Denton, F. T., B. G. Spencer | *Population and the economy* |
| Dickinson, J. P. (ed.) | *Portfolio analysis* |
| Wilson, D. J. | *Power and party bureaucracy in Britain* |
| Wabe, J. S. | *Problems in manpower forecasting* |
| Willis, K. G. | *Problems in migration analysis* |
| Farnsworth, R. A. | *Productivity and law* |
| Shepherd, R. J. | *Public opinion and European integration* |
| Richardson, H. W. | *Regional development policy and planning in Spain* |
| Sant, M. (ed.) | *Regional policy and planning for Europe* |
| Thorpe, D. (ed.) | *Research into retailing and distribution* |
| Dickinson, J. P. | *Risk and uncertainty in accounting and finance* |
| Hey, R. D., T. D. Davies (eds) | *Science, technology and environmental management* |
| Britton, D. K., B. Hill | *Size and efficiency in farming* |
| Buchholz, E., et al | *Socialist criminology* |
| Paterson, W. E. | *The SPD and European integration* |
| Blohm, H., K. Steinbuch (eds) | *Technological forecasting in practice* |
| Piepe, A., et al | *Television and the working class* |
| Goodhardt, G. J., et al | *The television audience* |
| May, T. C. | *Trade unions and pressure group politics* |
| Labini, P. S. | *Trade unions, inflation and productivity* |
| Casadio, G. P. | *Transatlantic trade* |
| Whitehead, C. M. E. | *The U.K. housing market* |
| Balfour, C. | *Unions and the law* |